# MORE LIGHT,
# MORE POWER

George Dance's St Leonard's Church, seen from Kingsland Road, 1816. The building on the corner of Hackney Road is one of the parish watch houses. Holywell Street was the old name for Shoreditch High Street.

# MORE LIGHT, MORE POWER

## An Illustrated History of Shoreditch

DAVID MANDER

LONDON BOROUGH OF HACKNEY

SUTTON PUBLISHING

Sutton Publishing Limited
Phoenix Mill · Thrupp · Stroud
Gloucestershire · GL5 2BU
in association with the
London Borough of Hackney.

First published 1996

Cover photographs: *front*: Cabs wait for fares in the bustle of traffic at the junction of Hackney Road and Shoreditch High Street in the early 1920s: *back*; The coat of arms of Shoreditch Metropolitan Borough Council, adopted in 1900.

**British Library Cataloguing in Publication Data**
A catalogue record for this book is available from the British Library.

ISBN 0-7509-1217-0

Typeset in 10/12 Perpetua.
Typesetting and origination by Sutton Publishing Limited.
Printed in Great Britain by Ebenezer Baylis, Worcester.

*For Ted Harrison*

*(1902–1991)*

Shoreditch Charity School, Kingsland Road and heavy traffic on the turnpike. An engraving by Robert Schnebbelie, 1810.

# CONTENTS

Entrance to Hare Court, 80 Shoreditch High Street, built by William and Mary Barnett in 1725 and closed by Jeremiah Rotherham & Co. Ltd in 1900.

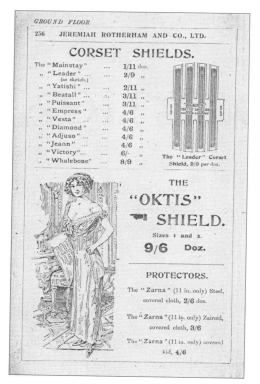

No lady could be complete without her corset shield.
From Jeremiah Rotherham & Co's hosiery range,
1914.

'To Islington and Hogsdon runs a streame of giddie people,
To eate cakes and creame.' Anon, 1623

'In fancy still where'er I roam,
I think of thee, my Hoxton home.' Anon, published in *Bentley's Miscellany*, Sept 1843

# Acknowledgements & Sources

All illustrations are taken from the visual collection at L.B. Hackney's Archives Department. The following are reproduced by kind permission of the bodies owning the reproduction rights: Bishopsgate Institute, page 85, 88 (bottom); Greater London Record Office, page 18, 33 (bottom), 42 (top), 69 (bottom), 77 (bottom), 78, 80 (bottom), 94; Hackney City Farm, page 125 (bottom); Hoxton Hall, page 82 (top); Mr A.H. Kay, page 82 (bottom); St Leonard's Church, Shoreditch, page 26 (top); Survey of London, page 5, 16 (top), 68 (bottom).

The author would like to thank Graham Reed who drew and designed the maps and Isobel Watson.

*Due to economic constraints, the sources for this book have unfortunately been omitted. A copy is available from the Hackney Archives and can be inspected in the Local History Collection.*

# 1. INTRODUCTION

Shoreditch, comprising some 640 acres, was the third smallest of the ancient Middlesex parishes. Since 1965 it has formed the southern part of the London Borough of Hackney, bounded to the south by the City of London, west by Islington and east by Tower Hamlets. Old Street crosses it from the west, and the Hackney Road makes up its south-eastern border. South of Old Street, development over the last hundred years has replaced residential streets with light industrial and wholesale premises, to the north much of the building developments of the period 1800–30 have been replaced with post-war council housing and parks.

Shoreditch's history has been extensively influenced by the adjacent City of London, and in the past it has had associations with holy and healthy water, Shakespeare and the Elizabethan theatre, as a place of quiet retreat to build almshouses and to incarcerate the mentally ill, as a place of discovery in medicine, plant nurseries and astronomy, as an alternative centre for drama, as a place of earnest nonconformity and grinding poverty, of real riches and industry, and false delusions of fanciful estates.

The first map of the parish was commissioned by the Shoreditch churchwardens in 1745 from Huguenot surveyor Peter Chassereau, and provides our introduction. Development had begun in the sixteenth century, but in 1745 buildings were largely confined to the south of Worship Street and along the principal roads. There were very few houses north of the present Cremer Street on the Kingsland Road, other than the three groups of almshouses on the east side; Haggerston was a small village around one manor house, with some houses round the other, just to the north of the Hackney Road. Hoxton Street was lined with houses, but Pitfield Street north of Fanshaw Street was little more than a path. For taxation purposes Shoreditch was divided into four liberties; Moorfields, Holywell, Church End and Hoxton, and these are now considered in more detail.

Moorfields lay to the south of Worship Street – the former Hog Lane 'called by their Worships Worship Street'. To the west lay the open fields of the Moor or Finsbury Fields, 'a dreary and unprofitable waste, consisting of one vast tract of morass, intersected by several ditches communicating with each other and most probably resorted to by the different kinds of wildfowl': so enthused Stow in the sixteenth century. From Worship Street ran the narrow Long Alley, flanked on the east and the west by common sewers. The majority of the liberty was built up by 1745, with just one open space which became Finsbury Market.

Holywell lay between Worship Street and Old Street. It was just to the north of Holywell Lane that Holywell Priory had stood, giving its name to the liberty, and to the main road. Development in this area included the early eighteenth century Webb Square, to the east of the High Street, and which was swept away in the mid-nineteenth century when Commercial Street was constructed. The line of the later Curtain Road petered out into market gardens which lay to the south of Old Street. Almost the only buildings on that turnpike road are the Agnes le Clair baths at the end of Willow Walk and Fuller's Hospital. North of Worship Street is Wittenoom's vinegar works and alongside it to the east is Holywell Mount. This had been raised as part of the Civil War defences of the City of London in 1642 and was claimed to have been a plague burial spot in 1665. It was a dangerous place as reports survive of robbery and rape in the mid-eighteenth century; and it was levelled in 1787 for development.

North of Jane Shore Alley lay the glebe land of Shoreditch Church, and here began Church End Liberty, which included St Leonard's Church; the watch house, and the site of Holywell Cross, first referred to in 1288. A medieval shop on the site, Smithes Forge, was demolished for road widening in 1768. The remainder of the liberty lay to the east of the Kingsland Road and included the open fields of Haggerston. From Hackney Road, Haggerston Lane ran north to the village and, as Slough Lane towards Stonebridge Common in Hackney. Haggerston village, which lay near the junction of How Street and Weymouth Terrace, also included the Burgoyne's manor-house whose lands covered northern Haggerston and was the birth place of astronomer Edmond Halley in 1656. The other manor, Hickmans, lay along the line of the Hackney Road, and the manor-house may have been on the site of the present Hackney City Farm. The Hackney and Bethnal Green boundaries were marked by small streams, and two footpaths crossed from the west; the northern making for the Shoulder of Mutton Bridge, and the southern, crossing at Watch House Bridge, near the end of the Row. On the footpath, in splendid isolation stood Goldsmiths' Almshouses, built in 1705.

The remainder of the parish came within the Hoxton Liberty, with the principal settlement on Hoxton Street. Much of the land between Hoxton Street and Kingsland Road was used for market gardening, although in the late seventeenth century there had also been flourishing plant nurseries in Hoxton. Hoxton Street had been a place of rural retreat and in the 1740s there were still many old houses of considerable size along both sides; one of the largest being the former manor-house which lay near the present junction of Hoxton Street and Pitfield Street. There was a bowling green, and rural taverns like the Robin Hood and the Rose and Crown. Perhaps the Rose and Crown's ale had its own peculiar properties, for the neighbouring lane was known as Sound Arse

Long Alley, looking towards the junction with Horse Shoe Alley from a watercolour by W. Broady, *c.* 1840. This area of Long Alley later became Finsbury Avenue. All the houses on the right hand side were demolished for the construction of Broad Street station in 1864–5.

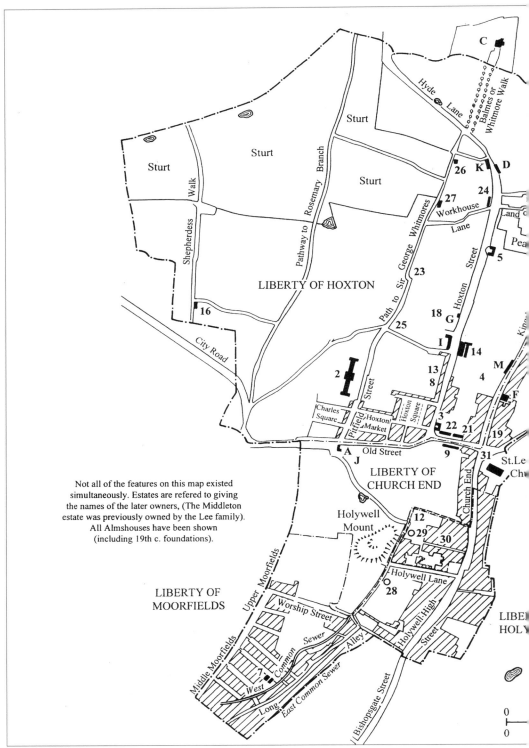

Shoreditch in the eighteenth century.

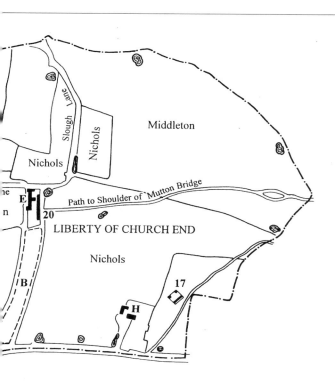

Middleton

Nichols

Nichols

Nichols

Path to Shoulder of Mutton Bridge

E F
20
n
LIBERTY OF CHURCH END

Nichols

B

17

H

ouses, Asylams and Workhouses
ermanbury Almshouses
e's Hospital (Haberdashers)
ger's Almshouse
man's Almshouses
rows or Holly House Asylum
rne's Almshouses
ch Almshouses
er's Almshouses
er's Hospital
ckney Road Almshouses
rwar's Almshouses
lier's Almshouses
xton Academy
xton House Lunatic Asylum
nmongers Almshouses (Geffrye Museum)
dy Lumley's Almshouses
rrell's or Goldsmith's Almshouses
d Gloucester St. Almshouses
reditch Charity School
reditch New Almshouses
lter's & Porter's Almshouses
tson's Almshouses
stby's Almshouses
Workhouse

Houses and Nurseries
A) St. Agnes le Clare
B) John Allports Nursery
C) Balmes House
D) The Bassano House
E) Burgoynes Manor House and Gate
F) Copt Hall
G) Haryong Family House
H) Hickmans Manor House
I) Leigh Family House
J) Nobles Nursery (approximate site of)
K) The 'Pitfield' House
L) George Rickets Nursery (site of)
M) Rotten Row

Public Houses and Theatres
25) Pimlico
26) Robin Hood and Little John P.H.
27) Rose & Crown P.H. and Sound Arse Al
28) Curtain Theatre
29) The Theatre

30) Hollywell Priory
31) Holy-Well Cross

2000          0.5ml.  3000ft.

0.5                              1km.

'The west entrance to the village of Haggerston' is the remains of what may have been the gateway to Burgoyne's manor-house, possibly on the east side of the later Weymouth Terrace. The engraving dates from 1794.

Alley in 1745. Just to the west lay the original parish workhouse. One footpath snaked its way north leading to the Rosemary Branch, while further east a second path passed Lumley's almshouse, built in 1672, on its way to Islington. This was Shepherdess Walk, crossing part of the prebendal manor of Finsbury and passing Wenlock's Barn manor-house.

This was Shoreditch in the mid-eighteenth century. Holywell had the most houses, 767 in total, but Moorfields with 630 was the most densely settled. Hoxton had 503 and Church End, the most rural, had 402. Within the next ninety years, development would cover the whole parish and Shoreditch's reputation as a place of rural retreat would be gone for good.

# 2. BEFORE 1660

Shoreditch lies just to the north of the City of London and, with two Roman roads running through the parish, would have been an early place of settlement. Just how early is difficult to tell, since most of the parish came within Stepney manor, held by the Bishops of London in the Middle Ages, and is not separately described in the Domesday Survey of 1086; only Hoxton and Haggerston are listed as individual places. The origin of the name Shoreditch is also uncertain. The earliest reference to 'Soerdich' is in around 1148, interpreted as meaning a ditch leading to the Thames. As late as 1745 two ditches still ran on either side of Long Alley. The derivations of other place names are more certain. Haggerston – 'Hergotestane' in Domesday – is probably the farm of Haergod, and Hoxton (or Hochestone, Hogeston, Hoggesdon and other variants) is the farm of Hogg or Hoc. Norton Folgate may have been the North Farm taking its second name from Richard Foliot, a canon of St Paul's in 1241. The manor of Wenlock's Barn is named after the thirteenth century Robert de Wenloc, of St Paul's Cathedral, who came from that Shropshire village.

There have been no prehistoric finds in the Shoreditch area, although there have been significant Palaeolithic (c. 450,000–12,000 BC) and Mesolithic (12,000–4,000 BC) flint tools found in Hackney and Stoke Newington. The Romans built Ermine Street through the parish to link London with Lincoln and York, and Old Street, the road to Colchester, crossed it. Excavations for an extension to the Geffrye Museum in 1993 uncovered a fourth century AD ditch running parallel with Kingsland Road. Otherwise there is little evidence of settlement patterns in the area until the Domesday survey of 1086. It is likely that the nucleus of Shoreditch village was around the Kingsland Road and Old Street junction. There is a tradition that a church stood there in Saxon times, but a grant for Shoreditch church by the Bishop of London to the Priory of Holy Trinity, Aldgate, between 1141 and 1149 is the first record. To the north, the canons of St Paul held two estates as Hoxton; one with three villagers, one plough team and pasture land, and the other with seven villagers and three plough teams. The second estate also had sixteen cottagers, who would have had little more than their dwelling and the small amount of land surrounding it. Excavations south of Nuttall Street near the Hoxton Street junction in 1993 found a medieval oven and other evidence of twelfth and thirteenth century occupation, suggesting that the medieval village of Hoxton lay at the north end of the street. The third settlement lay at Haggerston, where Robert Gernon held two hides, with land for two plough teams, three villagers and seven smallholders.

Dominating medieval Shoreditch's main street was the Priory of St John the Baptist at Holywell. It was a house of Augustinian canonesses, founded between 1133 and 1150 by Robert fitz Generan, who held the prebend of Finsbury or Holywell; his gift of three acres included the moor on which the Haliwell spring had its source. At the dissolution, Holywell Priory was the ninth richest of the English nunneries, with land in eight southern counties, although two thirds of the priory's income came from property in the City of London. Little of this came from royalty – Henry III had only given 300 tapers in 1239 and made good the damage to the priory's mills burnt down by the carelessness of his bakers five years later. But Sir Thomas Lovell, Chancellor of the Exchequer under Henry VII, was a notable benefactor who funded considerable building, including the chapel in which he was buried in 1524.

Lovell's funeral rites show the ostentation of the medieval way of death. The body was carried in a torch-lit procession from Enfield along Ermine Street to Shoreditch. At the entrance to Holywell Priory stood the Abbot of Waltham Abbey, the Prior of St Mary Spital, and the Bishop of London and his suffragan. The company then went through the priory church, the nuns' choir and into the great choir to sing a dirge, and 'during the said dirige there was a drynkynge in all the cloisters, the nones-hall and the parlors . . . for as many as wold come, as well as crafts of London, as gentilmen of innes of court, havyng wyne, beer, ale and ipocras, confits, spice bread, in good ordre; wich doone, every man went home for the night'. The following day there was a service of a hundred and forty masses and at last the burial. Offerings were made; hatchments put in place, and last but not least, over four hundred 'messes of mete' were served to those who attended.

Numbers of nuns varied between eleven and thirteen, with up to ten novices. There were lay brothers who worked with the nuns, and stewards who helped to collect rents. Most distinguished of the prioresses was Elizabeth Montague, in office by 1340, whose noble connections brought additional endowments. She was also vigorous in the defence of the Priory's rights, notably in 1356, when a group of armed intruders broke into the Priory, and abducted and married Joan, the daughter of John of Coggeshall, a former sheriff of Essex.

Holywell Priory was dissolved in October 1539, the fourteen nuns pensioned off, and the lands sold by the Crown. The priory site survived long enough to be included in Wyngaerd's sketch of London of about 1540, in which the high central spire of the church can be seen. Queen Catherine secured the site for her gentleman usher, Henry Webb in 1544 and the church and principal buildings were quickly demolished. Some outbuildings survived, including a gateway which was not demolished until 1785. As with many religious houses, the priory would have played an important part in the life of the local community and its passing must have signified the end of an era.

Although much of the priory had been demolished, the precinct survived and it was within the former priory grounds that Richard Burbage established The Theatre in 1576. Burbage was the head of the Earl of Leicester's Company of actors, who had given inn yard performances in the City of London. Faced with a ban on all play acting within the area of the City, Burbage had cast around for an alternative site, starting with the environs of his house, in Holywell Street. The former priory was the best option, and Burbage secured a twenty-one-year lease on part of the site, including the Great Barn. The Theatre was completed by the autumn of 1576. It stood on a site near the northern corner of the present Curtain Road and New Inn Yard, marked by two plaques today, and was probably an octagonal building. Despite troubles with his landlord and periods of closure due to plague, The Theatre survived for twenty-two years. However Giles Alleyn, the landlord, refused to renew the lease. Burbage died two months before it expired, in 1597. Just before Alleyn demolished it in December 1598, Richard's son Cuthbert Burbage, pulled the building down and carted the materials to Bankside, where they were reused to build the Globe on a site leased by Cuthbert, his brother Richard and five other actors, including William Shakespeare.

The Theatre was not the only early Shoreditch playhouse. The Curtain, probably taking its name from the priory walls, was built around 1578 on a site near the modern Hewett Street. Smaller than its rival, The Curtain may have been less successful, for in 1585 the owner Henry Lanman made an agreement with Richard Burbage and his brother-in-law to combine the two playhouses under one management. A variety of companies played The Theatre from 1590, including the Lord Admiral's Men, though by 1594 the Lord Chamberlain's Men were the chief company, including among their number Richard Burbage, William Kemp and Shakespeare. After 1596 the players moved from The Theatre to The Curtain.

William Shakespeare had originally joined Leicester's company and may have gone over to Lord Strange's Company after the death of Leicester in 1588. In the 1590s he lived in Bishopsgate. Some of his plays saw their first performance in Shoreditch, including *Romeo and Juliet*. Richard Burbage junior, a friend, was one of the stars of the new plays, being particularly celebrated as Richard III. On his death in 1619 he was buried in St Leonard's Church. However after the move to Bankside, the fortunes of The Curtain fluctuated – it was small and gradually deteriorating and could not compete with The Globe; it was demolished after 1627.

Shoreditch was famous for amusements other than the theatres in Elizabethan London. To the west of Hoxton Street were the common fields of Hoxton which, with Finsbury Fields were used for archery practice, regarded as important for national defence in the Tudor period. Henry VIII created mock titles for members of his guard

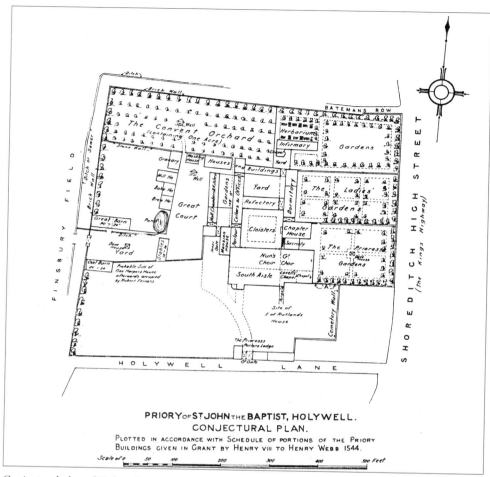

Conjectural plan of Holywell Priory.

A detail of 'The View of the City of London from the North towards the South' showing The Theatre on the left and the supposed flag of The Curtain playhouse on the right.

Richard Burbage, actor and theatrical manager,
c. 1567–1619.

who excelled themselves, starting with the 'Duke' of Shoreditch. The fields were also used for recreation, but local people wanted to farm them and there were attempts to enclose parts. There was a riot in 1498 when a mob from the City of London broke down hedges and ditches that had cut into the common. The fields were later marked out with wooden posts and stone 'rovers'. After a decline during the Civil War and Commonwealth period, archery was revived in the late seventeenth century as a sport; eventually the last archery society was incorporated into the Honourable Artillery Company.

Hoxton Fields were also a convenient place to settle quarrels. On 22 September 1598 dramatist Ben Jonson fought a duel with Gabriel Spencer, whom he killed. Jonson only escaped hanging by pleading benefit of clergy (proving he was able to write) and was branded instead. For the less strenuous there was always the tavern. One of the most famous was Pimlico, whose charms and good ale were extolled in a poem published in 1609 'Pimlyco, or Runne Redcap; 'tis a mad world at Hogsdon'. Pimlico gardens, which probably took their name from a kind of ale, lay between Pitfield Street and Hoxton Street, more or less due east of the present St John's Church.

The original settlements had been concentrated on Holywell Street and the junction of Kingsland Road and Old Street. Houses in this vicinity included the fifteenth century Copt Hall, on the east side of Kingsland Road; houses like this were later sub-divided as

The Robin Hood and Little John, Hoxton Fields and archers. Watercolour, possibly from about 1800.

the population grew. The tongue of land between Kingsland and Hackney Roads was already being used to make bricks in 1602, possibly for new developments like Ratcliffe or Rotten Row, twelve houses on the west side of Kingsland Road, built in 1614. But it was Hoxton, with its country airs that attracted the most prestigious development, as courtiers and foreigners sought relief from London. In 1568 the Portuguese ambassador had a house in southern Hoxton and opened his private chapel to allow English Catholics to join his household at mass. This brought along the parish constable and a colleague, but confronted by swords from the congregation and strong language from the ambassador, who called them 'vilians, dogges and such like', the pair had to beat a hasty retreat.

The proclamation of 1580 against the construction of new houses within three miles of the City of London was an indication of concern rather than an effective measure of control. By the end of the sixteenth century there were over twenty houses along what is now Hoxton Street, some known by sign names like the Golden Bull and the Red Lyon (not all of which were taverns!) Inhabitants included Jerome Bassano, whose father Antony, a Venetian, had been a musician at Queen Elizabeth's court. In 1598 the

Bassano house, on the west side on the site of the later Wilmer Gardens, was burgled and gold, jewellery and money worth over £100 stolen. The majority of these houses were on the east side and there were only three large properties on the west. To the south lay an estate which had belonged to Sir Humphrey Starkey, chief Baron of the Exchequer in 1484. After his death in 1486 successive sales saw it pass to the Leigh family in 1553. The house that went with the estate, on the site of the later Fanshawe Street, survived into the eighteenth century. The last occupant was probably Dr Daniel Williams, the nonconformist divine, who died there in 1715/16, and whose book collection went to form the nucleus of Dr Williams' Library.

To the north, on the site of the later Myrtle Street, was the house of the Haryong family, who are first recorded as Shoreditch residents in 1377. In the 1580s the house was occupied by Sir Thomas Tresham, one of the most notable of the Elizabethan Catholics. He was imprisoned in the Fleet in 1581 for harbouring the Jesuit Edmund Campion and later confined to a house near his Hoxton residence, where he was 'badly lodged . . . his chamber being allotted over a noisesome kitchen, rudely and disjoinedly boarded and not a whit ceiled'. During his lease his house was occupied by his son-in-law, Lord Monteagle, and it is likely that it was here, on 26 October 1605, that Monteagle received the letter warning him of the Gunpowder Plot, which led to the unmasking of the conspiracy.

At the top end of Hoxton was the house and estate of Sir Valentine Browne, bought before 1575. His estate later passed to the Roper family, who sold it in 1648 to Charles Pitfield (from whom Pitfield Street takes its name). The moated mansion house, which stood on the east side of Hoxton Street, near the site of St Ann's Church, was burned down in 1652. Rebuilt two years later, it must have been one of the grandest houses in Hoxton after Balmes, with thirteen hearths and a separate banqueting house in the garden.

A picture of one of the smaller Hoxton houses is given in the sale of 1618 of a house whose site later formed part of Hoxton House lunatic asylum. It had four rooms on the ground floor, with an old porch, and 'fower chambers and a garrett and three studyes or closetes in the said roomes' above. In front was a yard 18 ft by 9 ft, with a water pump, and at the back a 156 ft long garden with a summer-house. Tudor and Stuart Hoxton was indeed a pleasant place in which to live and play.

Civil War fortifications in Shoreditch. Two redoubts built on either side of Kingsland Road at the Hackney Road and Old Street junctions, as they might have appeared in the 1640s.

Old houses at the bottom end of Kingsland Road. Undated sketch from the late eighteenth century.

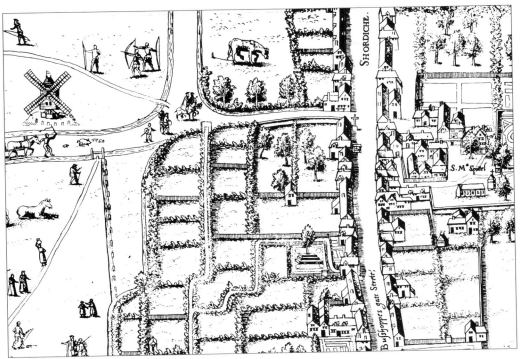

The southern end of Shoreditch in 1559, with archers on Moorfields.

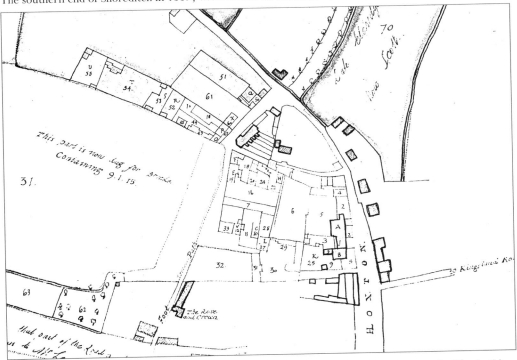

The north end of Hoxton Street in 1764. The present day Pitfield Street is still a path. The building marked 'A' is the rebuilt Pitfield House, although by this time it was a tenanted property on the Sturt estate and the banqueting house in the garden had probably been demolished.

The old St Leonard's Church from the south-west (above) and the east, in July 1735.

# 3. PARISH CHURCHES

The medieval church of St Leonard — the dedication is to a companion of the Frankish King Clovis, who became bishop of Limoges and died in 570 — was built initially of chalk and rubble, but later brick and stone, with a tile roof. It had four aisles, the last being a chantry chapel whose construction was funded by Sir John Elrington around 1482. The Elrington family also contributed to the cost of a painted glass east window, which included a figure of St George and Elrington's coat of arms. By the late seventeenth century the square tower at the west end, had been weatherboarded and held five bells, whose sound is said to have pleased Elizabeth I. Medieval images of the saints and the Virgin Mary were removed at the Reformation and three galleries were added between 1581 and 1630. Among the many who used the church were the players and musicians associated with The Theatre and The Curtain, and a monument in the present church commemorates the Burbages (father and two sons), players at the Rose and Globe theatres, and Richard Tarlton, one of Queen Elizabeth I's Players and the finest comic actor of his time. Gabriel Spencer, who came off worst from the duel with Ben Jonson was buried here, and the church was also the last resting place for Will Somers, court jester to Henry VIII, who died in 1569.

St Leonard's Church features in the nursery rhyme, 'Oranges and Lemons'. The rhyme was first recorded in the eighteenth century, though originally 'when will you pay me, Say the bells of Old Bailey' were answered 'When I grow rich, Say the bells at Fleetditch'; Shoreditch being a later replacement.

The old church was repaired in 1675, and again in 1700, when the chancel was raised and a new painted altar piece installed. Donated altar cloths were stolen immediately, by thieves who had hidden in wait in the church. But the repairs had not been enough — in 1711 the parishioners unsuccessfully petitioned Parliament for a new church. Two years later a great storm blew down part of the steeple, exposing two bells and on 23 December 1716: 'Last Sunday the church at Shoreditch giving a frightful crack, the audience, seeing a great deal of mortar fall down from the ceiling, ran out in such confusion that several persons were dangerously hurt in the crowd.'

Investigations revealed that the floor was 8 ft below the level of the adjoining street and confirmed that the building was in a very poor state. The bishop ordered the parish to either rebuild or thoroughly repair the church, but it was not until 1733 that a committee was appointed to view the fabric, whose report led to the preparation of a Parliamentary bill, becoming an Act in 1735. This authorised the creation of a temporary tabernacle in the churchyard, and the demolition of the old church. Work began in October 1735. Trustees were appointed to manage the project, and they selected George Dance the elder, whose new church, begun in November 1736, was completed in 1740. During construction, some of the labourers were sacked and cheaper Irish labour hired instead – Irish migrants were employed as casual labourers at harvest time. The result was a riot on three successive nights in which a public house kept by an Irishman was attacked; the Irish retaliated and the militia had to be called out to quell a mob estimated at 4,000 in number. With restrictions on Catholic worship, life could not have been easy for the migrants. In February 1735 the watch disturbed a hundred people gathered in a garrett at the back of a small alehouse near the High Street to celebrate mass. The priest had to escape and names and addresses were taken, but the more determined of the congregation met there again in the evening to reconvene the disrupted service.

The new church incorporated some monuments from the old, together with the bells. The 'London Scholars', an ancient society of bell ringers, had their headquarters in the church and were renamed the Royal Cumberland Youths, by the Duke of Cumberland, in recognition of the peal rung in his honour in 1746 after his return from the defeat of the Jacobites at Culloden Moor. New features included two fine bread cupboards, in which fifty loaves were placed each Sunday for the local poor up to the 1870s. The panels of the doors are made of slats cut to give a diamond pattern. The organ, built by Richard Bridges in 1756, and rebuilt in 1913, was one of the casualties of bombing. The church was affected by an incident at nearby Calvert Avenue in 1940 and also by a flying bomb in 1944. The organ, though damaged, was repaired and converted to electricity, but the 1940 blast destroyed all the windows, including a fine Te Deum window, dating from the early seventeenth century and made of Flemish glass. This had been taken down by the vicar, John Squire, and buried during the worst of the Puritan excesses in the Commonwealth period. Restored after 1660, it had been removed during the First World War in anticipation of bombing. Funds were not available in 1939 to repeat the process, and none of the glass was saved.

In the churchyard is the Clerk's House, which dates from 1735. Before the church was rebuilt there was a corresponding house on the other side of the church, which had provided accommodation for the chantry priest before the Reformation. This and a house on the site of the Clerk's House were the subject of a dispute at the end of the sixteenth century, which was eventually resolved when both were assigned to the vicar; to be used to lodge the minister or schoolmaster or parish clerk and for church meetings. The house on the corner with Hackney Road had been the vicarage. Rebuilt by vicar John Squire in 1631, it was demolished in 1784 and the site taken for a watch house. As a replacement the parish bought a house in Hoxton Square, where subsequent vicars have lived. The churchyard, closed for burials in 1857 was taken over by Shoreditch Borough Council and maintained as a recreation ground, along with the additional burial ground on Hackney Road. Among the surviving monuments is one inscribed '1807, Dr John Gardner's Last and Best Bedroom'! The parish stocks and whipping posts survive under a rustic cover.

Despite the tremendous growth in population in the late eighteenth and early nineteenth centuries, St Leonard's remained the sole Anglican church until the mid-1820s. Then, with the assistance of the Church Building Commissioners and the Metropolis Churches Fund, two new churches were built to serve parishes carved out of St Leonard's – St John's Hoxton in 1826 and St Mary's Haggerston in 1827. Two further churches were built in 1839, two more in 1848 and from 1855 to 1875 a further thirteen churches. Four of these were the work of architect James Brooks, including the massive St Columba's on Kingsland Road. All were designed to be cheap, but also tall and conspicuous. There was a battle for religious attention to be fought in nineteenth century Shoreditch, and many of the poorest parishes were Ritualistic; notably St Augustine's Yorkton Street, consecrated in 1867. It was to the newly-formed St Augustine's parish that an Anglican order of nuns came in 1866, after their first house in Ash Grove, Hackney had been broken up by the conversion of some members to Roman Catholicism. Under their first superior, Mother Kate, St Saviour's Priory was to play an important in the social and religious life of Haggerston, as we shall see in a later chapter.

Declining populations from the 1930s brought about two church closures. Four churches were either destroyed or bomb damaged and a further eleven churches have been closed, as parishes have been merged. Some survive in use by other faiths, as with St Columba's, or in secular use, like St Augustine's.

The interior of St Leonard's Church, a view looking towards the altar of 1895. The east window was one of those lost in the Second World War bombing.

St John the Baptist Church, from Pitfield Street. A lithograph by C.J. Greenwood in 1854. Funded by the Church Building Commissioners, the church was largely designed by Francis Edwards and was consecrated in June 1826. There have been many later alterations and considerable repairs were needed after bomb damage in the Second World War. The church survives today, although it was closed for worship in 1988 and the parish merged with St Leonard, Shoreditch.

Interior of St Paul's Church, Broke Road, Haggerston, as seen by the *Builder*, 31 March 1860. This was the first church designed by the architect A.W. Blomfield.

St Mary's Church, Haggerston. Engraving of 1837. The church received a direct hit in 1940 and was destroyed.

St Columba's Church, Kingsland Rd, *c.* 1905. Designed by James Brooks in 1869.

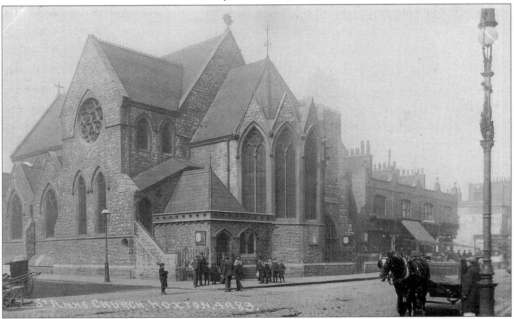

St Ann's Church, Hoxton Street, *c.* 1905. Designed by Francis Chambers, it was built in 1868–9.

# 4. MINISTERS, MULCH & MORTAR: 1660–1840

The proximity of the City of London provided the stimulus for market gardening, and by 1633 John Noble had six acres of garden ground between Old Street, Willow Walk and the High Street, where he grew fruit trees and asparagus. The growth of London after 1660 encouraged the development of town gardens and Hoxton was a good locality for plant nurseries, with plenty of garden ground close to the potential market. Probably the first nurseryman was George Ricketts, who was established to the north of the present Nuttall Street by 1665, producing flowers (tulips were a speciality), fruit and lime trees as well as evergreens for ornamental tubs. By the 1690s he had a reputation for high prices and poorly cared for stock and his nursery, mortgaged by his heir in 1711, did not survive long after his death. Adjoining was Pearson's nursery, specialising by the 1690s in anemones 'which he would only sell to gentlemen'. Unlike Ricketts, Pearson had no greenhouses, and he protected his myrtles, striped Philareas and other greens from frost by use of sheds and straw cover. A small garden was kept by William Darby from around 1677, whose specialities included *Fritilaria crassa*, with a flower 'the breadth of half a crown, like an embroidered star of several colours'. Darby also grew striped hollies by pollination and collected exotics, including the Great or American Aloe and the Torch Thistle, which flowered for his successor. He kept a pressed leaf and flower collection, although it was his successor, John Cowell, who published some account of his activities in *The Curious and Profitable Gardener* of 1730.

But the most notable of the Hoxton nurseryman was Thomas Fairchild, who

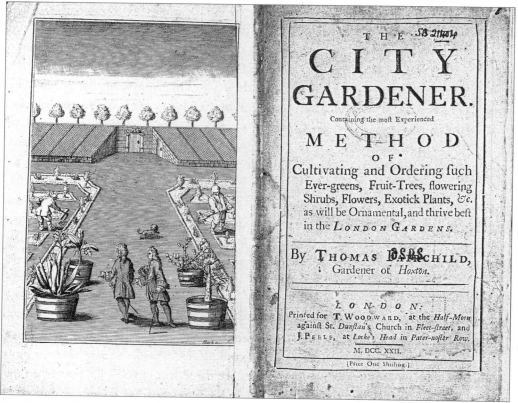

Frontispiece to *The City Gardener* by Thomas Fairchild, 1722.

produced the first artificial hybrid plant, *Fairchild's Mule*; a cross between a carnation and a Sweet William. Starting up in around 1691, he was noted for his vineyard and botanical experiments. His *The City Gardener* of 1722 offers advice on gardening from window boxes to the planting-out of a City square. Fairchild's friend and near neighbour, Benjamin Whitmill, also published seasonal advice in *The Gardener's Universal Calendar*, which first appeared in 1726. Fairchild's nursery was carried on by his nephew until his untimely death in 1734. Taken over by John Simpson, it finally closed in 1740. By then the great days of the Hoxton nurseries were over, as land was taken for building and the smoke from London chimneys increased. John Allport's nursery, west of the later Weymouth Terrace in Haggerston, was still trading in 1805, but this was the very last of the pioneering nurseries that have earned Shoreditch a place in gardening history.

House building prior to 1660 was mainly concentrated on existing roads and in the south of Shoreditch. Existing houses were replaced by tenements or supplemented by new houses on their gardens, as would appear to have happened in Cock Lane (later

Boundary Street), when the 'Cock in the Hoop' – already divided into two – had seven neighbouring properties added by 1615. The uncertainties of the Civil War period and the Commonwealth that followed may have impeded building, though in 1658 an estate to the north of the present Drysdale Street was being dug for brick earth.

Major development of the area to the north of Old Street began in the 1680s. The former Leigh estate, which had passed to Sir Edward Massie, was sold in two blocks. Isaac Honeywood bought land near Old Street in 1677, and leased part of it out to Antony Ball and John Brown in 1683. They in turn sub-let to Charles Hill, who may have been responsible for the layout of Charles Square in 1685 and who in turn sub-let a plot to William Charles. It has been assumed that one of this pair was responsible for the name of the square, but the original names of the surrounding streets – James (now Boot Street), Queen (Coronet Street) and King (later Rufus Street), would suggest general naming from the Stuart royal family. Honeywood sold part of his holdings to the Haberdashers' Company in 1690 and this formed the site of their hospital and school. The remainder of the estate was leased to Samuel Blewitt and Robert Hackshaw in 1683 who laid out Hoxton Square. By 1730, when the freehold had been sold to Israel Wilkes, father of the radical politician John Wilkes, there were over a hundred houses, a nonconformist chapel and the London Apprentice public house on the estate; which included King Street and the frontages to Hoxton Street. Charles Square was not built up immediately. Only the north and east sides are dated from 1685–90; houses on the east side were completed around 1726, while the south side remained empty until 1770–4.

In the next thirty years all the remaining open space to the south was developed, the tangle of courts grew ever more crowded and older houses in Kingsland and Hoxton were demolished to make way for smaller properties. In 1788 the Shoreditch Trustees for the Four Rates complained of 'the very great number of small houses that have lately been builded in the parish'. By 1801 the population of Shoreditch stood at 34,766; in twenty years this rose to 52,966 as building spread out from the old roads – Kingsland Road, Hoxton Street and the line of the modern Pitfield Street. Construction of New North Road opened up the fields of north-west Shoreditch to the builder and by 1825, development on the Sturt estate between New North Road and Bridport Place was under way, with streets were being laid out south of the Regent's Canal towards Shepherdess Walk and the spoil tips of the dust contractors. William Rhodes leased the estate north east of the present Hyde Road in 1803, with the farm buildings fronting onto the site of the present roundabout with Pitfield Street. Rhodes was the lessee of the De Beauvoir estate further north and had completed development on the Shoreditch estate by the 1820s before he began work to the north of the Regent's Canal in Hackney. Between Bridport Place and Pitfield Street, there were still market gardens, but these were soon to be swallowed up in Hoxton New Town. To the south, one of the last areas of open space was the estate immediately around Aske's Hospital. The Haberdashers' Company had already developed their lands to the east of Pitfield Street – this section of the road was known as Haberdashers' Walk – and two short roads had been laid out at the beginning of the nineteenth century. However the decision to demolish the old hospital in 1822, allowed the Company to use less of the site for their new building, and build over the fields and gardens at the rear; laying out Buttesland and Great Chart Streets and completing the present Bevenden Street to join East Road.

The largest landowner to the north-west were the Sturt family, who had come into the Pitfield estates through marriage in 1756; the descendant of this marriage, Lord Alington still held the freeholds in 1917. The Sturts had also acquired a neighbouring estate belonging to John Mobbs through foreclosure of mortgages. Mobbs had kept his children in ignorance of his affairs and in the 1830s, one grandson, William Mobbs, made a series of attempts to claim title to the estate. He issued a grand proclamation and instructed 'his' tenants to withhold rent from the Sturts. The case became celebrated locally as 'Mobbs Millions', and looked to have the potential of a *Jarndyce* v. *Jarndyce*, but Mobbs failed to prove his case and died in poverty. But for many years thereafter Mobbs' descendants continued to carry out research, convinced that the 'millions' were there for the taking.

One of the smaller Shoreditch estates belonged to the Pearson family; one part comprising land to the south of Shoreditch workhouse between Kingsland Road and Hoxton Street and the remainder, Crab Tree field and part of Nicholls' fields on the east side of Kingsland Road, at the rear and to the north of the Ironmongers' Almshouses. Though the main road frontages had been developed much earlier, only the western end of York Street (later How Street) had been completed by 1802. It is possible that the intended development was delayed by a slump in 1825, but Pearson Street was laid out three years later and the remainder of the estate by the mid-1830s, with streets named from family associations (Maria Street from Michael Pearson's wife, Fellow Street from his sister-in-law). The field to the south of this part of the Pearson estate remained a market garden until 1841, when it was laid out as Nichols Square, to the design of John Henry Taylor.

Haggerston was the last area of Shoreditch to be built over. Much of the medieval estate of Hickmans had come into the hands of Richard Nicholls in 1726. By 1812 Dove Row and Margaret Street to the east of Goldsmith's Row had been completed and within eight years William Rhodes was laying out streets between Haggerston Lane and Goldsmith's Row, and making tiles near the later Tuilerie Street. In 1814, Haggerston was described as 'proverbial for depravity', with a large population of brickmakers, although a recently established school was said to be having a good effect. The construction of the Regent's Canal encouraged further industrial development and a large site was taken by the Imperial Gas Company in 1823.

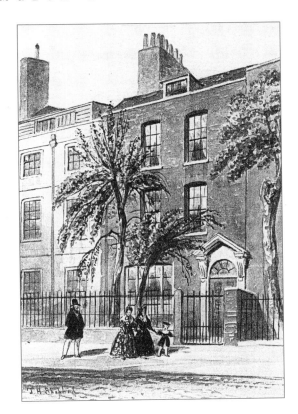

No. 36 Hoxton Square, the former vicarage.
Watercolour by T.H. Shepherd, *c.* 1844.

Part of the Burgoyne's estate had been purchased by Robert Lee from Oliver
Cromwell in 1598. It passed to the Lee family, then to the Actons. Development begun
under Nathaniel Lee Acton, who, seeing the potential for industry along the newly-
formed Regent's Canal, obtained an Act of Parliament in 1808 allowing him to grant
leases long enough to attract builders. Leases for plots in Acton Street were granted in
the same year, though major development waited until the 1840s under the ownership
of Sir William Fowle Fowle Middleton. His surveyor George Pownall, after whom one
of the roads on the estate is named, laid out a gridiron pattern of streets which fitted
with the neighbouring development of William Rhodes. Better class housing was
reserved for the area north of the canal, stretching into Hackney; to the south, industry
was mixed with housing.

All this development took place within a local government system unchanged in
broad essence since the sixteenth century. The parish was not merely religious in
significance; from the sixteenth century onwards many local administrative duties had
been laid on it to perform, including care of the roads and the poor. The governing
body was the vestry, elected by a variety of means. In Shoreditch an 'open' vestry,

where all inhabitants could have their say, had given way in 1730 to a 'select' vestry of the more prosperous inhabitants. This body chose who could join their ranks. The vestry made a selection of potential holders of the elected offices of churchwardens, overseers of the poor and surveyors of the highways. In both closed and open vestries the only scrutiny of parochial accounts was by the Justices of the Peace, and it was alleged that in the early eighteenth century the local justices put self interest in evading paying rates before their duty to ensure that the parish was well run. As a result Shoreditch's affairs were put before the main Quarter Sessions in 1691 and 1743, and in 1744 one parishioner felt so strongly about the matter that he produced a lengthy pamphlet. In the later part of the century, the closed vestry gave way to an open meeting.

To be fair to Shoreditch, some of their expenses were not of their own making. Two major roads ran through the parish – Ermine Street, from Bishopsgate, through Shoreditch High Street and north along the Kingsland Road, and Old Street. Local people were having to contribute their own labour and money to repair nationally important roads. In 1713, Shoreditch joined with six other parishes to petition Parliament on the state of Ermine Street, claiming that it was 'so worn out by frequent travelling therin that it is very dangerous in the winter season'. As a result an Act was obtained, that created a trust to appoint surveyors and rate collectors, dig drains, extract gravel from private lands and collect tolls from newly-erected gates. Shoreditch and Hackney agreed to levy rates as a substitute for the enforced or statute labour. The Stamford Hill Trust, established in 1713, was followed by other turnpike trusts. The Old Street Trust, set up in 1753, also managed Curtain Road and Worship Street. Hackney Road formed part of the Hackney Turnpike Trust of 1738. Trusts were also set up to build new roads: City Road, constructed in 1761, and New North Road, authorised in 1813, built by 1823. These main roads were the haunt of highwaymen, so it was a natural extension of the work of the trusts to take on street lighting and provide watchmen. But complaints of delays at the toll gates and of the varying rates charged were perennial. There were gates at the west end of Hackney Road, at the junctions of Old Street and Curtain Road, in the middle of Worship Street and at the top end of the Kingsland Road, in Hackney. Varying standards of road maintenance and the all too numerous proliferation of gates led to the formation of the Metropolis Roads Commission for all turnpikes north of the Thames, in 1827. But the new body retained the areas of the old trusts and did not rationalise tolls. It also attempted to deal with the problem of new streets off roads like Kingsland Road, by erecting new side gates, causing further resentment. It was not until 1863 that the Metropolis Roads Act abolished the Commission, and with it all the gates, returning roads to parish control.

Turnpike Trusts were an example of the ad hoc bodies being created to deal with problems of local administration that the vestry felt were beyond its means. There were others — a trust was created to 'enclose and embellish' Hoxton Square in 1776, extinguishing the residual rights of common and putting up iron palisades round the centre. Separate acts passed between 1737 and 1768 created no less than three bodies concerned with road repair, lighting and watching, of which the largest was the Trustees of the Four Rates for Repairing the Highways, whose minutes survive from 1778. This body also controlled the parish watch, built wooden watch houses, provided the watchmen with guns and greatcoats and tried to ensure that they stayed awake and sober. The watch was abandoned in 1829, when its functions were taken over by the newly formed Metropolitan Police, one of the first London-wide bodies.

To one seventeenth century satirist Hoxton was synonymous with nonconformist meetings but from the end of that century it also trained many ministers for chapels throughout the country. There were four successive training colleges, the first three known as the Hoxton Academy. The first was founded in 1699 through the patronage of William Coward, a merchant whose wealth came from the West Indies trade, and who lived in Walthamstow. This was a Presbyterian foundation, initially established at

The south side of Hoxton Square in the 1920s. Houses on the west side have been replaced by warehouses. The fate of No. 31 is typical; a school room was built at the back in 1809, which was leased to a chairmaker in 1849, and later extended.

The London Apprentice, Old Street. This photograph of 1894 was taken just before the old building was demolished for the present one.

The west side of Charles Square, showing No. 16. This had been Shoreditch County Court from 1847, and had a passageway entrance from Old Street. It is now the London regional headquarters of the Labour Party, and is the only original building remaining in the square; all else having been demolished by Shoreditch Council. Postcard of about 1900.

No. 3 Fanshaw Street, formerly the Hoxton watch house. Built in 1819 in what was then Robert Street, it was passed over to the Metropolitan Police in 1829 and was still in use as a police station in the early 1850s. The building was demolished after the Second World War.

Hoxton Academy Chapel, Short Street, after rebuilding in 1856.

Coventry. When it closed in 1729, the Academy buildings remained vacant until taken over by a second academy, which had started in Wellclose Square, Stepney, and moved to Hoxton in 1762. This was Congregational, though both the principal tutors, Rees and Kippis tended towards Sociniasm, and doctrinal disputes eventually led to closure in 1784. Possibly the most famous pupil of this period was William Godwin.

The third Academy, training Independent or Congregational ministers, moved from Mile End into the vacant buildings in 1791. The principal tutor was Robert Simpson, who founded the Hoxton Academy chapel in Short Street in 1796. The chapel was rebuilt in 1806 for a congregation of up to 1,500. A Sunday school, opened at the rear in 1814, claimed to be the first purpose-built one in London. It was to remain an active force in Hoxton religious life through the nineteenth century, outlasting the Academy, which shut its Hoxton premises in 1830 and moved to Homerton. A fourth training college, this time for Methodist ministers, used the old buildings from 1834, sending some students to Abney House in Stoke Newington. Both sites were to close in 1842–3, an infectious epidemic among the Hoxton students hastened the end, and the Hoxton Academy premises seem to have passed into industrial use. The last link in

Hoxton Academy Sunday school, Hoxton Street, 1920.

successive nonconformist effort was ended in 1941 when the Sunday school was destroyed by bombing.

Huguenots worshipped in a chapel near Hoxton Square from around 1714 to 1785; not far away in Bath Street was the original site of the French Hospital, catering for poor and sick members of the community. Opened in 1716 it moved to Victoria Park Road in Hackney in 1866. Foreign nonconformists might be tolerated, but some home-grown preachers had problems finding anywhere to worship. The revivalist preacher George Whitfield used the open Moorfields to attract huge crowds from 1739 and he also held a mass meeting in Charles Square in 1742. A year before, John Wesley had held a similar service there and rowdies attempted to break it up by unleashing a bullock, but the animal merely circled the crowd and dashed off, leaving Wesley rejoicing and praising the Lord. It is not recorded whether Whitfield did the same when

Worship Street Baptist Chapel, on west corner with Long Alley, seen in a watercolour by T.H. Shepherd, *c.* 1843. Built with a bequest from the will of Isaac Jemmett, the chapel was completed in 1779 and used initially by four congregations. Affected by the conversion of some of its members to Unitarianism, the chapel lasted with diminished membership until 1878, when it was demolished for the construction of the Metropolitan Railway in 1878. A successor congregation still worships at Winchmore Hill.

one of his opponents climbed a tree on Moorfields overlooking his temporary pulpit and emptied the contents of a pot over his head.

Whitfield was spared further indignities when a wooden shelter was built for him in 1741; eventually in 1753 this was replaced by the Whitfield Tabernacle, just outside the Shoreditch boundary, on the corner of the eponymous Tabernacle Street and Walk. In 1853, dissension in Whitfield's Tabernacle led to the foundation of the New Tabernacle just south of Old Street and west of Charlotte Street; this building survives today, refurbished as a business centre. Whitfield's original church was rebuilt in 1868. It survived the Second World War and closed around 1956.

By the end of the eighteenth century there were Baptist and Methodist chapels in Shoreditch providing vigorous competition for the Anglican church, which was slower to respond to the population explosion that was to follow with the development of the area in the ensuing thirty years.

The original Whitfield's Tabernacle, Tabernacle Walk. This was built in 1753 and seen here shortly before demolition in 1867.

Nos. 46–8 Hoxton Street. Watercolour by Evacustes Phipson, 1919. Built after 1680 on the former Star Close, these houses were among the last survivors of the larger Hoxton domestic buildings, and had formerly been part of a larger house used as the Orphan Working School. By 1921 No. 48 was a children's welfare centre and both houses were demolished around 1935 for the construction of Castlefrank House.

The south side of Nichols Square showing the mixture of terrace and paired houses. A view dating from shortly after 1945, as the surface bomb shelter is still in place. Nichols Square was regrettably demolished in 1963 by Shoreditch Council as part of its comprehensive house clearance policy.

The Middleton estate north of Regent's Canal. Regent's Row is in the foreground, with Ipswich Road leading northwards. In the middle right distance is the roof of Pownall Road Congregational Church. The majority of houses in this view were cleared for the Regent's Court estate shortly after this picture was taken in 1957.

# 5. CHARITY & SICKNESS

In the years 1833–5 John Ware conducted a survey of Shoreditch's various parochial benefactors and found 116 gifts, ranging from almshouse charities, to donations of a pulpit cloth and cushion. The earliest dated from 1581; medieval gifts would have been linked to chantries, with prayers for the deceased donor, and all of these were swept away in 1547. Charitable bequests were common to all Anglican churches, but Shoreditch's proximity to the City of London, combined with its suburban charms, made it an ideal location for the almshouses and as late as 1850 there were no less than eighteen in the parish, but many were to vanish in the ensuing two decades and only one set of buildings now remain.

The Reformation ended the belief in the giving of alms for remission of the soul from Purgatory, but from the mid-sixteenth century there were more bequests intended to help the poor, many from City of London merchants. The Statute of Charitable Uses in 1601 improved the administration of charities and contributed to greater generosity in the ensuing forty years. This was interrupted by the Civil War, the Commonwealth years, and financial pressures on the merchant community in the reigns of Charles II and James II. After 1688 the flow of gifts increased, with donors able to establish a school or an almshouse and make provision for an income to maintain the foundation for the future. But from the 1690s donations could be made through subscriptions to some of the newer bodies, like the Society for the Propagation of Christian Knowledge or to older hospitals for the sick. Almshouses were less appropriate for subscription funding, since gifts could only be used for pensions of the almspeople, salaries of officials and the maintenance of the buildings, and there was a gradual decline in new foundations after 1735. It was not until the beginning of the nineteenth century that there was a revival in interest in almshouses, leading to the rebuilding of some and additional endowments for others in the period up to 1850, after which the fashion for 'giving' was to change again.

The history of almshouses in Shoreditch reflects this pattern. The earliest was

Weavers' Almshouses, north side of Old Street. Watercolour by T.H. Shepherd, *c.* 1844.

established under the will of John Fuller, a judge and sometime Treasurer of the Inner Temple, whose will of 1592 directed that two almshouses be built; one in Stepney for twelve men, and the other, for twelve women, in Shoreditch. Fuller's widow acquired a site on the south side of Old Street and built the almshouses before 1605, adding a further endowment before her death in 1623, though the almshouses were not incorporated as her late husband had intended until 1680. Fuller's Hospital, administered by Shoreditch Parish, was rebuilt in 1787 and moved to new buildings in Wood Green in 1865 when the site was taken for the construction of a fire station and a town hall for Shoreditch Vestry.

    Shoreditch parish ran three other almshouses. Badger's Almshouses, at the south-east end of Hoxton Street, were in a charitable huddle with three other foundations – the Refuge for the Destitute to the rear, Weavers' Almshouses to the south, and Walters' and Porter's Almshouses to the south east. Founded under the will of Allen Badger in 1674, the almshouses were built in 1698, accommodating six women until demolition in 1873. Hackney Road almshouses were converted from an engine and watch house built in 1825 in the grounds of the additional churchyard laid out in 1625 on the north side of Hackney Road. Appropriately it was intended that two of the four old almsmen should have been former watchmen for the parish. After the creation of a united Shoreditch parish almshouse at Wood Green, the Hackney Road buildings were demolished in 1904 and the site is now a playground. The last parochial foundation, the Shoreditch New Almshouses, founded in Kent Street, Haggerston in 1852 for twenty locals, lasted until just after the Second World War.

The most impressive foundations were set up under the auspices of the City Livery Companies. Aske's Hospital in Pitfield Street was established by the Haberdashers' Company under the will of Robert Aske, dated 1689. Established by an Act of Parliament, the charity acquired the Pitfield Street site, and invested the balance of the bequest in lands in Kent. Robert Hooke designed the first buildings, which were completed in 1695. The foundation housed twenty poor freemen of the Company and a school for twenty sons of freemen. After the development of the grounds for housing, the original buildings were demolished in 1822 and replaced by a range designed by David Riddell Roper, completed in 1827. Changes in the charity during 1873 led to the closure of the almshouses and expansion of the school; Shoreditch Vestry then prevailed the London County Council to house Shoreditch Technical Institute there from 1898.

Along the east side of Kingsland Road, there were three foundations. South of the present Geffrye Museum were Harwar's Almshouses, founded in 1704 and managed by the Drapers' Company. The Geffrye began as the Ironmongers' Company almshouses, built in 1712, with a small central chapel, and to the north lay Bourne's Almshouses founded under the auspices of the Framework Knitters' Company in 1734. The Drapers' Company administered Walters' and Porter's Almshouses on the site of the present Old Street Magistrates Court. These had been founded in 1656 under the terms of the wills of John Walter and his widow Alice. Originally catering for eight almspeople, jointly appointed by the Company and Shoreditch parish, the almshouses were extended through the gift of Thomas Porter in 1826 and the entire site rebuilt. Adjoining and to the east were the Weavers' Company almshouses built on land leased from the parish for 200 years in 1669. These seem to have gone on the expiry of the lease. Last of the Livery Company foundations was Richard Morrell's foundation, built in the fields of Haggerston in 1705 for poor members of the Goldsmiths' Company on the path which was to become Goldsmiths' Row. Although in poor repair in 1863, the almshouses lasted until 1889, when the combination of building costs and the poverty of the surrounding area led the Company to sell the site for redevelopment and divert the charity into pensions.

The parishes of St Botolph's Aldgate and St Botolph Bishopsgate, were left funds by Elizabeth, Viscount Lumley for an almshouse in 1657, but took fifteen years before admitting that they could not find a site in either parish. In 1672 they used a site on the

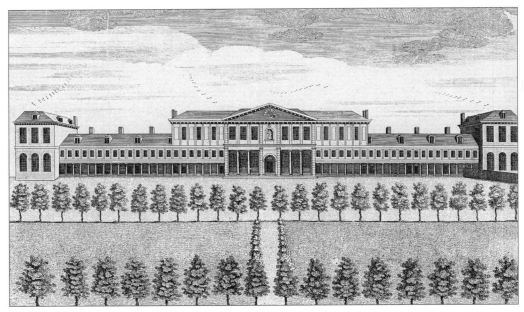

The east front of the original Haberdashers' Almshouses. Early eighteenth century engraving by B. Cole.

east side of Shepherdess Walk and the resulting foundation, rebuilt in 1822, lasted until 1898. Other almshouses with religious associations included Berman's Almshouses, founded by a Presbyterian minister for eight women in 1703. The original almshouses, east of Hoxton Street, were replaced by buildings in Basing Square, off Kingsland Road, in 1813.

Another almshouse with Presbyterian associations was founded by Mrs Mary Westby and her sister in 1749. Westby's Almshouses, on the east side of Pitfield Street, south of Bacchus Walk, lasted until 1881, when the site was taken for a board school. They were originally for protestant or dissenting widows or spinsters, and were known locally as 'The Old Maids' Almshouses'. Prior to 1865 there was an almshouse founded by the Dutch Church in London, between Crown Street and Whitecross Alley. Built in 1688 for poor church members, the site was acquired by the London and North Western Railway in 1865 and the foundation moved to Charlton in Kent.

Some of the parochial donations included land and houses in Shoreditch parish, others funded gifts of bread or money to apprentice local children. Of the many donations, two have lasted until modern times. Thomas Fairchild, the Hoxton nurseryman, left money in his will of 1728 for the preaching of an annual sermon at Whitsun on either 'The wonderful works of God in Creation' or 'On the certainty of the resurrection of the dead, proved by certain changes of the animal and vegetable

The second Haberdashers' Almshouses, as drawn by T.H. Shepherd, 1828.

The west front of Lumley's Almshouses, Shepherdess Walk and their gardens. Built in 1672, these buildings were replaced in 1822. This engraving was published in 1834.

The Dutch Almshouses, Mulberry Court, Whitecross Alley. A watercolour by T.H. Shepherd, 1843. The almshouses were on three sides of a court facing onto a small green and stood there until 1865.

Berman's or Bernander's Almshouses, Basing Square, looking west with the grounds of Hoxton House lunatic asylum to the rear, in about 1920. Nearby Basing Place was bombed in March 1941 and it is likely that these buildings were destroyed then.

Bourne's Almshouses, Kingsland Road. A watercolour by T.H. Shepherd, probably dating from the 1830s. The small wooden hut at the north end of the almshouses looks like an unrecorded turnpike toll house. Bourne's Almshouses closed in 1907 when the foundation moved to Oadby in Leicestershire and the almshouses were demolished.

Morrell's or Goldsmiths' Almshouses, on the west side of Goldsmiths' Row. Another T.H. Shepherd watercolour from the 1830s.

Shoreditch Charity School, Kingsland Road.
Watercolour by T.H. Shepherd, about 1840.

parts of creation'. Known locally as 'The Vegetable Sermon', Fairchild's bequest was observed until recent years. John Dawson, an exciseman, left a substantial library in his will of 1763. The majority of these books survive, in the care of Hackney Archives Department, and Dawson's library is one of the few remaining parochial libraries left in London.

The education of the poor was also left to charitable foundations. The parish's own charity school opened in 1705, funded by subscriptions from each of the liberties, catering for fifty boys chosen from the different areas of Shoreditch in proportion to the funds each contributed. Beginning in a room in Pitfield Street, the school later moved to a house at the south east end of Kingsland Road. A girls' school was opened in 1709. Donations funded clothing for the pupils, which often ended up being worn by their parents. There were no great aspirations to high academic standards – the goal was apprenticeships for the boys and domestic service for the girls. In 1799 widening of the Kingsland Road provided the opportunity and some help with the funding to build a new school on the same site. The foundation of other schools in Shoreditch in the 1830s

The Orphan Working School, Hoxton Street. A view from about 1840.

gradually diminished the importance of the charity school, though it did not close until 1889. The school building of 1799 survives as a betting shop.

Orphans had an even tougher time than the parish poor. In 1758 a group of nonconformists established the Orphan Working School in a small house in Hoxton Street, initially taking in twenty boys, but later admitting twenty girls; again with the objective of apprenticing the boys and training the girls to be domestic servants. They would appear to have taken over a complete house (part of which survived to become 46–8 Hoxton Street) but the age of the Hoxton property led to the school moving to new premises on the south side of City Road in 1775. It was to remain there until 1847, when the end of the lease enabled the governors to move their 240 charges to Haverstock Hill. In 1988 the school was at Reigate, called the Royal Alexandra and Albert School.

Shoreditch's own poor were catered for in the parish workhouse from 1726, when one was built on the west side of Hoxton Street, between Ivy Street (originally Workhouse Lane) and the later Hemsworth Street. Among the bequests the parish received was a gift of an estate on the opposite side of Hoxton Street, called the Land of Promise. When a lease came up for renewal in 1776 the eastern half, including the Kingsland Road frontage were passed over to the newly-created Trustees of the Poor to build a new workhouse, completed in the following year. Workhouses also catered for sick as well as healthy paupers, and after a succession of parish doctors of varying ability, the parish was lucky to secure the services of James Parkinson and his son in 1813. The Parkinsons initiated improvements in the care of the sick, including the separation of surgical from medical sick, the establishment of a maternity ward and the isolation of fever cases. The last reform was given impetus by the typhus outbreak of 1815 which spread through the courts and alleys of Hoxton, and Parkinson's fever block was the first of its kind in London. In a later outbreak, only five people died, such was the success of the new policy. Parkinson had produced a pamphlet on parochial fever wards, but it is for his *Essay of the Shaking Palsy*, which appeared in 1817 that he is remembered today, through the illness that now bears his name, Parkinson's Disease.

There was little immediate change with the creation of the new poor law in 1837, since after only the briefest of intervals, the Shoreditch Board of Guardians was abolished, with control reverting to the Trustees of the Poor, who had managed poor relief since 1774. The Trustees protested against the edicts of the government's Commissioners of the Poor to abolish relief given outside the workhouse, to reduce bread and beer rations for inmates, and wholly dispense with their beer. In 1847 the lease on the western half of the Land of Promise came up for renewal and the parish was able to build a new range which included a kitchen, bakehouse, fever hospital and infirmary. An artesian well, sunk in 1850, provided fresh water. Fit pauper men were put to work breaking stones in a yard opposite the Britannia Theatre, south of Falkirk Street.

By 1851 the older buildings were becoming decrepit. There were 718 inmates in that year, over half of whom were over sixty-four years old, and sixty-four of whom were children. Some pressure was relieved by the despatch of pauper children to a new parish school at Brentwood from 1852, but more space was still needed. Shoreditch's new vestry, formed in 1856, promoted a local act, which saw the abolition of the trustees in 1858 and their replacement by an elected board of guardians. A major rebuilding programme was launched in the 1860s to cater for the increasing numbers of the poor in better conditions. The site of the 1777 workhouse was cleared. Offices and a boardroom for the guardians were built on the Hoxton Street frontage in 1863, alongside the stub of a lane that had once led to the Land of Promise. The Kingsland Road block was rebuilt in 1866 and accommodation for 1,200 inmates, including separate accommodation for the sick was finished by 1862. By 1871 there were sixty

The Kingsland Road frontage of Shoreditch Workhouse, from a watercolour by T.H. Shepherd of about 1840. Built in 1777, this building was demolished to make way for a new block, completed in 1866.

more inmates than in 1851, but a growth in medical staff reflected the improved treatment for the sick. Nursing staff included Edith Cavell, who was Assistant Matron from 1903 to 1906 and who was in Brussells in the First World War. Accused of helping wounded soldiers escape, she was executed by the Germans in October 1915. When the workhouse finally closed in 1930, the whole site became St Leonard's Hospital, which closed as a general hospital in the late 1980s. Redevelopment in the 1990s has left only the façade of the old Guardians' Office on Hoxton Street, incorporated into the offices of a housing association.

Not all City of London parishes chose to look after their own poor, making arrangements instead with private institutions to farm out their paupers. In 1811 Jonathan Tipple took a lease of the Great White House (or St John's House). This had been built on the east side of Hoxton Street as the residence of Oliver St John, third baron Bletsoe in 1610. From about 1740 to 1760 it was a boarding school kept by the father of minister George Baddeley. In 1814 Tipples, and a neighbouring house run by

St John's House, kept by Thomas Tipple, a pauper farmer from an engraving of 1823.

Mr Robertson were inspected for a Parliamentary enquiry. Robertson's was dirty, overcrowded, without provision for the sick and with pigs running about in the pauper exercise area. Both Tipple and Robertson relied on income from pauper labour to support their houses. St John's House was still taking City paupers in 1823, but in its last period was divided into rooms for the local poor, with one room used for a Wesleyan Methodist Bethesda Chapel. It was demolished in 1845 to build Henry's Place.

Shoreditch, and especially Hoxton were to gain a reputation for crime in the nineteenth century, and so it was appropriate that the Refuge for the Destitute, established in Lambeth in 1806, moved to a site to the west of the present Cremer Street in 1811. The Refuge was founded to aid and reform discharged prisoners. Initially both sexes were accommodated at the Hackney Road site but a grim barrack-like block was opened behind Badger's Almshouses on Old Street for men alone in 1815. In the early days the Refuge also took in prostitutes, but soon limited aid to ex-

The Male Refuge for the Destitute looms grimly behind Badger's Almshouses on Hoxton Street. Watercolour by T.H. Shepherd, about 1840.

convicts. Men were given work, which included tailoring, shoe and basket making and wood chopping; all of which helped with funds. As part of its intention to provide a new life for inmates, the Refuge sent eleven boys to South Africa in 1817, but it was not until 1832 that a major programme of emigration was begun, with young single women sent out to Australia and men to Australia, Canada and the United States. The work of the Refuge had been assisted by a government grant and when an eight-year-old black boy, Tom Alert, was rescued from a slave ship in 1846, he was sent to the Refuge. But when the grant was reduced and then withdrawn after 1849, the Refuge closed the male establishment, which was sold to an upholsterer, and moved the women, then numbering forty, to the 'Manor House' on Dalston Lane in Hackney.

But it was not for the poor that Hoxton was best known. As early as 1672 the poet Andrew Marvell declared an opponent 'fit for nothing but Bedlam or Hogsdon', for as Hoxton began its social decline and the rich abandoned the large houses, some became lunatic asylums. Hoxton House, which lay just to the south of St John's House, was an asylum from 1695, and was run from about 1715 by the Miles family, who enlarged the site in 1784. No qualifications or medical training was required, though it was common for owners of asylums to call themselves apothecaries, as William Prouting did in 1710. He declared that he had taken over the house of the late Claudius Gillett, which had 'all the conveniences [and] fittings for such Persons as a large House, pleasant Gardens . . . and gives Liberty to any Physician, Surgeon or Apothecary of administering Physick to those that are recommended it'.

The most notorious of the Hoxton asylums was Whitmore House, rebuilt for Sir George Whitmore around 1635. It was acquired by Richard de Beauvoir in 1687 but when his son bought an estate in Essex, the house was no longer needed and by 1756 had become an asylum run by Meyer Schomberg. After passing through various hands, including John Silvester, a former military doctor, it passed through marriage into the hands of Thomas Warburton. Warburton was involved in the concealment of a young officer, John Mitford (a cousin of Lord Redesdale, ancestor of Nancy and the other Mitford sisters), in 1812–13, when Mitford was in hiding after involvement in a perjury case, and allowed his involuntary guest free range of the house. In his *A Description of the Crimes and Horrors in the interior of Warburton's Private Madhouse* published thirteen years later, Mitford left a vivid description of the living conditions of the mentally ill from wealthy families.

Warburton himself was an imposing six foot, with a huge three-inch nose and great strength, who had risen from door keeper to owner of the house. Patients were given only an annual medical inspection by one Dr Willis, and much of the money given for their keep was taken by Warburton and his keepers. Inmates could be beaten and confined to dark cellars, while women could also be raped or prostituted. Little of the suffering of patients, who included the son of Henry Addington, (prime minister, d. 1823) and the Duke of Atholl (d. 1846) was recorded. As Dr Willis was called in to Windsor to care for George III, Warburton and his crew also came along, using rough treatment and blows to restrain the King. It is not surprising that George III could not bear to look at Warburton and used to exclaim: 'Take away that fellow with the long nose – take him away, away, away!'. Warburton also used small houses in Hoxton to farm out some of his inmates, like the four room house in Ivy Lane, which in 1819 housed an inmate to each room, plus a keeper in 1819. He also had larger establishments at Bethnal Green for paupers who were mentally ill, where conditions were even worse than at Whitmore House.

The trade in lunacy was the subject of a Parliamentary Select Committee in 1815 and the introduction of licensing brought in some improvements and a fine for the associate of Warburton's responsible for the Ivy Lane house. Sir Jonathan Miles, summoned before the Committee in 1815, had enlarged the Hoxton House buildings in the previous year and some improvements may have ensued. It was here that Charles and

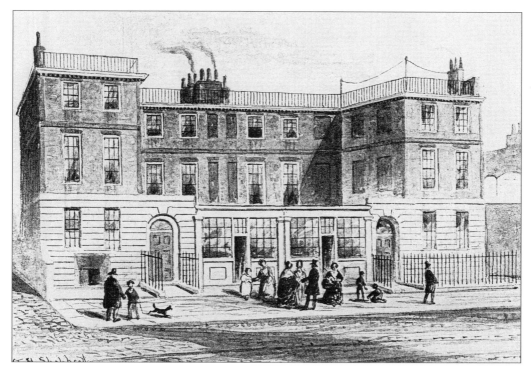

Burrows or Holly House. Watercolour by T.H. Shepherd in the late 1830s.

Mary Lamb were confined, and one local recalled meeting Charles, describing him as 'a little Bob Cratchit of a man . . . with a neat frail body carrying a large head that looked somewhat top-heavy'. Warburton's houses in Bethnal Green featured in a further Parliamentary enquiry of 1827, which led to statutory regulation of metropolitan madhouses under the Metropolitan Commissioners in Lunacy; the first stage of significant Victorian reforms.

Nor were all houses as bad as Warburtons. Burrows, or Holly House, established by 1791 in Hare Street, between Hoxton Street and Kingsland Road, seems to have had a reputation for humane treatment, helped no doubt in that the visiting surgeon was James Parkinson. In 1819 the building was old and overcrowded, though it seems to have been rebuilt, before being demolished for redevelopment around 1840.

Parkinson had been one of those who pressed for two doctors to take part in each certification, to prevent false proceedings and legislation and to improve conditions. Warburton himself escaped retribution, and it was the mental illness of his own grandson combined with the value of the land which led to the closure of Whitmore House and redevelopment of the site in 1851. Hoxton House, rebuilt and losing part of

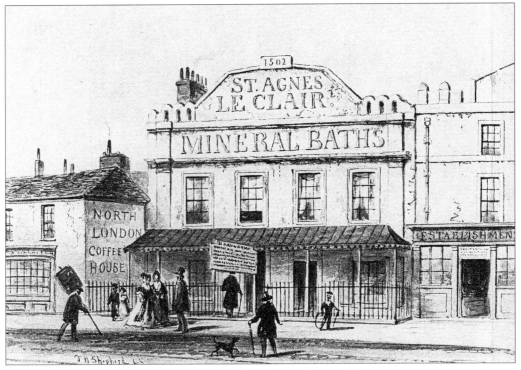

St Agnes Le Clair Baths, Old Street. Watercolour by T.H. Shepherd, 1843.

its site, lasted until 1902, and the tall red brick house that survives on Hoxton Street today was once part of the last of Hoxton's lunatic asylums.

Shoreditch played a small but important part in the history of inoculation. The tradition of health giving waters had lingered on after the passing of the Holy Well. Water from St Agnes Le Clair well, on the north-east side of Tabernacle Square, was supposed to cure rheumatism and nervous disorders, and in the sixteenth century there was a bath for each sex, fed from a spring 18 feet below. The well became a spa bath in the eighteenth century, lasting until a fire destroyed the building in 1847, though industrial use of water in the area must have begun to affect the water table by that date. It may have been the close proximity of the spa bath that attracted the promoters to take a house nearby, on the north side of Old Street, in 1746 as one of three premises forming a subscription-funded hospital to vaccinate against smallpox; the others being used to isolate infected patients and for general purposes. The Old Street house, marked by a swan in relief, taken from a house destroyed in the Great Fire of London, remained in use until 1754.

There were two important hospitals in Shoreditch. The Royal Chest Hospital was

# GREAT REDUCTION
## *In the Prices of Cold and Warm Bathing!*

THE ONLY BATHS FOR THE ESTABLISHMENT OF HEALTH & THE CURE OF ALL
NERVOUS AFFECTIONS AND COMPLAINTS OF THE SKIN ARE THE

## COLD, WARM, VAPOUR AND SHOWER
# BATHS.

FROM THE CELEBRATED & ANCIENT CHALYBEATE SPRINGS OF
# ST. AGNES LE CLAIR,
### *Tabernacle Square, Finsbury,*

Which are ALWAYS READY from five in the Morning till eleven at Night, and may
be used by Persons of either Sex, at any Season of the Year,
without the liability to Cold.

| Cold Baths. | | | TERMS. | Warm Baths. | | |
|---|---|---|---|---|---|---|
| Ladies and Gentlemen ℙ Ann. | £1 | 5 | 0 | Single Bathe | £0 | 2 | 0 |
| Three Months | 0 | 15 | 0 | Twelve ditto | 1 | 0 | 0 |
| Two Months 12s. .. One Month.. | 0 | 8 | 0 | Vapour ditto | 0 | 4 | 6 |
| Single Bathe | 0 | 1 | 0 | Six ditto | 1 | 4 | 0 |
| Shower, One Month | 0 | 15 | 0 | Shower, One Month | 1 | 1 | 0 |
| Single Shower | 0 | 1 | 0 | Single Shower | 0 | 1 | 6 |

THE Proprietor begs to inform the Public, that he has at a very considerable ex-
pence, fitted up several Warm, Vapour, and Shower Baths, in addition to the spa-
cious Cold Baths, for Ladies and Gentlemen, the whole of which form one of the
most convenient Establishments in or near the Metropolis, and the ONLY ONE OF
ANY REAL BENEFIT in Rheumatic and Nervous Affections, Determination of Blood
to the Head, violent Head-Aches, Scorbutic and Cutaneous Eruptions, Erysipelas,
&c., as can be testified by numbers that have received speedy Cures.

They have been carefully analyzed by several eminent Professional Gentlemen,
and are especially recommended by the Faculty to Persons confined by Business
during the day, and to growing and delicate Youth; for such they are peculiarly
efficacious, as, by equalizing the circulation of the blood, they are the means of
preserving Health; and, by promoting Perspiration and the various Secretions,
they allay Nervousness, remove Disease, and impart a regular stimulus throughout the whole System.

These Springs are constantly flowing at the rate of *Ten Thousand Gallons every twenty-four
hours,* and possess the singular property of remaining at all Seasons of the Year *at the same mode-
rate temperature.*　　　[G. HANCOCK, PRINTER, BUTTESLAND STREET HOXTON.

St Agnes Le Clair promotional leaflet, *c.* 1840.

City of London Lying-In Hospital, City Road, 1907.

funded in 1814 in City Road, the first hospital in Europe to specialise in chest diseases and what was then called consumption. Rebuilt in 1863, it was expanded in 1876–7 for out-patients and further building work followed in the next forty years, including the acquisition of the site adjoining Providence Chapel in Regent Street in 1901. Acute problems prompted a merger with the Royal Northern Hospital in 1919; the hospital closed prior to 1956 when Shoreditch Council acquired the site for housing. The City of London Lying-In Hospital was founded in 1750 and moved to the City Road corner with Old Street in 1771. By 1900 a third of its patients came from Shoreditch, benefiting from the care generously supported by funding from City of London sources. Rebuilt around 1908 it later changed its name to the City of London Maternity Hospital, moved to Tollington Park around 1956 and closed in the 1980s. Shoreditch people were also able to use the Metropolitan Hospital, which had been founded in Lincoln's Inn Fields in 1836 and moved to the Hackney part of the Kingsland Road in 1886. Active fund-raising by local worthies, including garden parties, helped rescue it from early difficulties and it survived as a general hospital until 1975, finally closing in 1977. It is now in use as workshops.

# 6. 'A MODEL VESTRY'? 1855–1900

By 1851 the population of Shoreditch had reached 109,257 and it was to peak ten years later at 129,364. The bulk of this growth had been in Hoxton and Haggerston, and although the Rhodes development in Haggerston and parts of the Sturt estate in Hoxton New Town contained some better houses, the bulk of what had been built was mostly two storied terraced cottages. As building regulations were minimal, much of this housing was poor quality and the bulk of it still had no provision for sewerage in 1856. In the cholera epidemic of 1849, 889 people died in Shoreditch. Density of population was also increasing. There had been clearances to the east of Shoreditch for the building of the Eastern Counties Railway terminal (later Bishopsgate Goods station) in the late 1830s, but the construction of the North London Railway extension to Broad Street in the early 1860s caused even more problems, especially as increasing industrialisation in south Shoreditch saw the take-over and replacement of domestic property by factories, warehouses and showrooms.

The Metropolis Management Act of 1855 attempted to bring some degree of order to the bewildering methods of electing vestrys and created the first governing body for London, the Metropolitan Board of Works. Local particularism at the time was especially strong, so none of the plethora of small parishes were amalgamated, and all nominated members to the new MBW. The Act created new standards for the regulation of building control, drainage and public health, and created a framework for the MBW to undertake some major construction works, including new thoroughfares to improve the flow of London traffic. But it was the local vestries, often barely changed from the old parochial ones, that had to shoulder the majority of the burdens of improving conditions within their areas.

The limits of the franchise ensured that the bulk of Shoreditch's vestrymen were tradesmen, though they were not so parsimoniously inclined as some of their colleagues in other authorities. There were 120 of them and although meetings were often poorly attended they could be noisy, rowdy affairs. In 1881 one paper reported that the ratepayer 'who, explaining why he had heard nothing of a great thunderstorm, said he was at a meeting of the local vestry' was assumed to be a Shoreditch resident. There were two loose political groupings, one for parochial reform, and the other grouped round a ratepayers' association. The latter held power in the early 1870s, but in the main the reformers were in command – although neither group maintained a continued existence in the manner of a modern political party. In the first ten years Shoreditch Vestry was an active body which undertook extensive paving and sewerage works, built a new town hall on Old Street in 1865–7, and, under the auspice of an active medical officer of health, Dr Robert Barnes, set up an effective system of notification of diseases, backed up by inspection. Barnes and his inspectors sought to abolish cesspools, repair drains, remove refuse and provide ventilation. The question of the water supply was also tackled – water supplied by the East London Water and New River Companies was impure and inadequate in quantity. Under these poor conditions, the death rate stood at 28 per 1,000 per year.

Barnes' efforts also extended to the regulation of cowhouses and slaughterhouses, and to the control of industrial pollution; the closure of the ancient burial grounds in 1857, the watering of streets and the erection of public urinals. These were not always welcome – in 1872 inhabitants of Shoreditch High Street were to petition against one at the junction of Commercial Road as a traffic hazard and a potential affront to female sensibilities – but taken together Shoreditch's actions resulted in the death rate dropping to 23.5 per 1,000 in 1864. Two years later the outbreak of cholera in East London was contained in Shoreditch, which proved itself to be one of the most vigorous of the London vestries, appointing twelve medical visitors, and only 170 people died.

However the initial impetus was not maintained. The deterioration in housing stock, demolitions and continuing influx of immigrants from outside London, combined with the loss of 650 houses and displacement of 4,500 people by the North London Railway works began a noticeable decline in living standards. The problems of overcrowding were made worse in 1867, when the Ecclesiastical Commissioners cleared 650 houses on their estate on the Shoreditch–St Luke's borders and let the sites to the Improved Industrial Dwellings Company. This had been set up by Sydney (later Sir Sydney) Waterlow, who had vastly expanded his family's printing business to become Waterlow & Sons. Sir Sydney's first project, Langbourne Buildings in Mark Street (named after the City ward he served as an alderman), was built in 1863. Both it and the later projects were intended to provide housing for the better off members of the working class and yield a five per cent dividend. Shoreditch Vestry was to complain that the tall blocks badly affected the light in neighbouring streets, and they and other observers also noted that the rents charged were beyond the means of those people displaced by the developments, who had to seek accommodation in the older, and increasingly more crowded surrounding streets and courts. In Hoxton the richer contingent moved away as overcrowding worsened. In Hoxton Square some houses held seven or eight households in 1871, while one house, divided into two, had no less than fifty people living in eleven households. Tiny Barton Court, off Hoxton Street, had ninety-nine people in eighteen houses in 1851; twenty years later this had doubled to 184.

Dr Barnes had left in 1868 and his successor, Dr Henry Gawen Sutton, who was to remain in the post until 1891, documented the increasing social problems, but seems to have failed to take the imaginative action needed. This may have been due to the influence of Enoch Walker, a former vestryman and journalist, who became vestry clerk in 1870 and remained in post until his death in 1890. Walker was more interested in street improvements. Commercial Street had been completed to Shoreditch High Street in 1858; Walker was also instrumental in cajoling the MBW to extend its line through to Old Street to form Great Eastern Street in 1876. He was also behind the widening of the west side of Shoreditch High Street at the north end in 1877, and, despite some local opposition, in creating Appold Street to replace Long Alley in 1879. Shoreditch was one of the few vestries to have regulations to control overcrowding in multiple occupancy houses, but enforcing orders in court proved difficult. Hackney had solved the problem by raising rents – but this only caused further problems for neighbouring Shoreditch. National legislation existed to govern the closure of unfit property – the Torrens Acts of 1868 and 1879 – but owners could always claim that they were going to carry out repairs, even if this was not the case. Nor had the vestry made any progress with provision of baths and washhouses. The old vestry had adopted the Baths Act of 1846 and even purchased a site, but its successor had abandoned the project and twice refused to consider the large expenditure required.

A change of attitude began in the mid-1880s. The area returned two radical MPs in the election of 1885, William (later Sir) Randal Cremer for Haggerston and Professor James Stuart (active in the promotion of popular education) for Hoxton. The vestry surveyor was dismissed on the grounds of advanced old age in 1887, and three years later H.M. Robinson took over as the new vestry clerk. Robinson ensured that the vestry managed refuse collection and street cleaning instead of contractors, improved rate collection and initiated some major projects. These included major sewer reconstructions, the acquisition of the first public open space in Shoreditch (other than the cleared old graveyards) in Goldsmith's Square and the adoption of the Baths and Washhouses Act. Public Library Commissioners were established and took over the former offices of the Independent Gas Company on Kingsland Road to become the first public library, opened in 1893. The Shoreditch Technical Institute, the first of its kind in London, was established in 1893 in Hoxton to train workers for the furniture and building trades. With the support of the London County Council (which had replaced the MBW in 1889), it moved to the former Aske's Hospital in 1898. Extensive local unemployment prompted the creation of a labour bureau. Pressure on the LCC combined with new legislation enabled Shoreditch to undertake a major housing scheme, clearing houses in the vicinity of Nile Street to create the Provost Street housing estate in 1898; linked to the LCC's new construction of Vestry Street. The Provost Street scheme was the first public housing undertaken by a vestry in London. On the public health front the old urinals were replaced with underground toilets; and, with the expansion of staff, the town hall was enlarged.

But the vestry's major achievement was the proposal to provide a library, baths and washhouses, an electricity generating station and refuse destructor on one site. Heat from burning the rubbish would provide power for the generators and enable the vestry to supply electricity to the whole of Shoreditch. In 1891 Shoreditch became the second London authority to acquire the right to generate electricity and the second in the country to provide it, when the entire scheme was completed in 1899, opening on the site of the former Middlesex Ironworks in Pitfield Street. The vacated houses attracted thieves, wanting to remove fireplaces and the like. Robinson's solution was to hire Jack Knifton, a local boxer, who garrisoned the site with some like-minded friends and for several weeks beat off the local toughs, until clearance could be completed. In the first five months of its operation the electricity undertaking made a profit equivalent of 5.5 per cent. Much still remained to be done, but when the former Prime Minister, Lord Rosebery, opened the Provost Street housing and was given a guided tour of the municipal glories of Pitfield Street in 1899, he was able to praise Shoreditch as 'one of our model vestries'. A new metropolitan borough was to take over in 1900, with its motto 'More Light, More Power'; drawn on the greatest achievement of its predecessor.

The vestries had no direct responsibility for primary education, although the parish had run a charity school since 1705. The Board of Guardians provided a school at Brentwood for pauper children, opened in 1854, providing training in carpentry, painting, tailoring, shoemaking and baking for boys, with the less able working on the farm. Girls were taught basic domestic skills, intended to equip them to become servants. Enlarged in 1870 the school was jointly used by Hackney and Shoreditch from 1877 until 1885, when Hackney Poor Law Union took over.

Both Anglican and nonconformist churches had provided Sunday schools from the late eighteenth century. A Wesleyan Sunday school was built in Ivy Lane in 1832, and another in New North Road in 1864. The first Anglican National School opened in an alley off Munday Street in 1822, supported by voluntary subscriptions, fees, grants and offertory sermons. Christ Church opened its national school in 1839 and St John's Hoxton in 1842. In 1851 there were 144 private schools in the parish, compared to

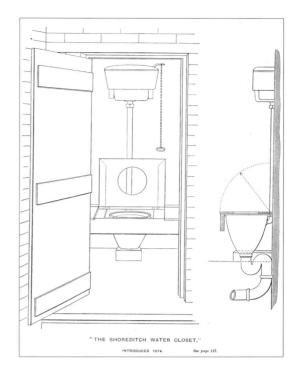

"THE SHOREDITCH WATER CLOSET."

INTRODUCED 1874. *See page 117.*

The Shoreditch Water Closet. Designed in 1874 by Shoreditch's Chief Sanitary Inspector, Hugh Alexander, it was the first in the country not to be boxed in, and so could be easily cleaned.

Bishopsgate station, the terminus of the Eastern Counties Railway, as photographed by John Penarti in 1863. Opened in 1840, it closed when Liverpool Street station opened in 1874 and was rebuilt as a goods station in 1881. Most of the goods station was destroyed in a fire in 1964.

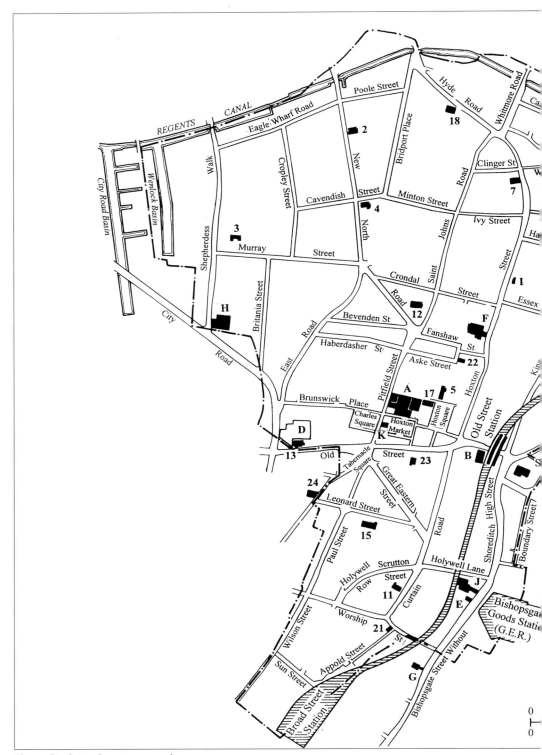

Shoreditch in the nineteenth century.

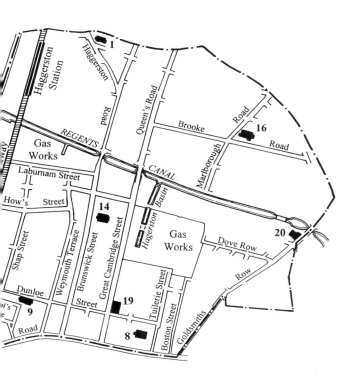

Churches
) All Saints' Church
) Christ Church
) Holy Trinity Church
) New North Road Methodist Church
) St Monica's Church  (Roman Catholic Chapel)
) St Andrew's Church
) St Ann's Church
) St Augustine's Church
) St Chad's Church
0) St Columba's Church
1) St James' Church
2) St John the Baptist's Church
3) St Mark's Church
4) St Mary's Church
5) St Michael's Church
6) St Paul's Church
7) St Peter's Church
8) St Saviour's Church
9) St Saviour's Priory
0) St Stephen's Church
1) Worship Street Baptist Chapel
2) Hoxton Academy Congregational Chapel
3) New Tabernacle
4) Whitfield's Tabernacle

Public Buildings etc
A) Library, Public Baths and Electricity works
B) Shoreditch Town Hall
C) Shoreditch Workhouse
D) Vinegar Works

Theatres
E) Alhambra Music Hall
F) Britannia Theatre
G) City of London Theatre
H) Grecian Theatre and Eagle Tavern
I) McDonald's (Hoxton Hall)
J) National Standard Theatre
K) Variety Theatre

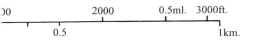

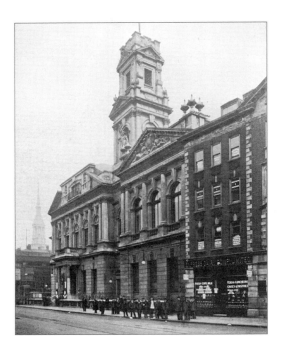

Shoreditch town hall was built on the site of
Fuller's Almshouses in 1865. The increased
activity of the vestry led to overcrowding, with
staff using the committee rooms. An extension
designed by W.G. Hunt was begun in 1901; this
view shows the completed building in around
1905.

Among the nooks and crannies of older housing
was No. 5 Queen Square, a narrow court on
the west side of Finsbury Avenue (once Long
Lane). This view catches the respectable W.H.
Brooks, chimney sweep, at his front door
around 1920, but the house did not always have
such a good reputation. In 1892 it was under
observation by the police and Shoreditch as a
suspected brothel. Each floor was occupied by a
separate family; with two women and their
children using the first floor. The Children's
Aid Society had already removed the children
before the ensuing prosecution.

The widening of Shoreditch High Street led to the demolition of property on the west side. This watercolour by J.P. Emslie shows the yard of Nos. 136–7, with the spire of St Leonard's Church rising above the cleared site to the north.

Typical of the narrow streets off Hoxton Street was Ivy Walk. This view of about 1920 was taken at the point where Ivy Walk divided into two; looking east to the narrow passage that led through to Hoxton Street. The houses on the left of the passageway would have had semi-basement rooms. All except the eastern stub of Ivy Walk (previously Ivy Lane), was cleared in the mid-1950s and the site forms part of the grounds of Macbeth House.

Shoreditch opened its first library in the former Independent Gas Company offices owned by the Gas Meter Company in 1892 (left). Four years later the building was extended (right).

Pitfield Street, showing the library and the matching baths to the south around 1905. Both the library and the baths, completed in 1899, were bomb damaged in the Second World War. The library was refurbished and re-opened in 1955; the baths were demolished after the war. After giving long service to Shoreditch people, Pitfield Street Library closed in 1995 in advance of the new public library, scheduled to open in 1997 within the Hackney Community College further up the road.

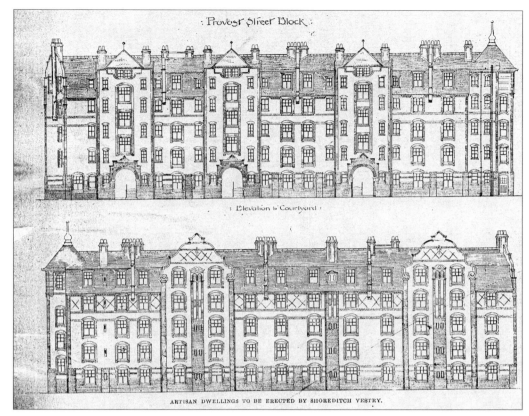

Elevation for the Provost Street housing scheme of Shoreditch Vestry, the first public housing built by any London local authority other than the London County Council. Designed by Rowland Plumbe, the work was linked to the construction of Vestry Street and completed in 1900.

nine Church of England National Schools, seven British Schools (predominantly nonconformist in origin) and one Catholic school. There was a Ragged School, founded in Phillip Street in 1846, which moved to a site in Hammond Square in Hoxton in 1850, donated by H.C. Sturt. By 1872 there were also Ragged Schools at Union Walk, Sclater Street and on Dove Row, in the poor district of Goldsmith's Row and while two preparatory schools still traded in Hoxton Street, the area was rapidly becoming too poor to support private schools. Future provision lay with the School Board for London, created under the Education Act of 1870. Although the School Board did not seek to compete with the voluntary sector, it often built its new schools in close proximity to them. By 1896 there were four Board schools in Hoxton alone, enlarged by the London County Council after 1904 and the church schools either closed or were absorbed by the LCC to take advantage of building grants.

St John's Schools, Hoxton dated from 1842, with an infant school added in 1848. The large classrooms were not suitable for later nineteenth century teaching and were modernised in 1908. This view from that year shows the new north frontage of the altered school.

Shoreditch Technical Institute included domestic economy classes in its course programme. This view shows one in progress at the newly-opened workshops in Buttesland Street in 1905.

# 7. POVERTY

'Hoxton is the leading criminal quarter of London, and indeed of all England', claimed Charles Booth, describing the area in the late 1890s. By then the overcrowding, clearances and industrial changes to south Shoreditch had altered the social composition of the whole area. The population, which had peaked in 1861 at 129,364, dropped gradually to 124,553 in 1891 and the better off gradually moved out. Nichol Square, where Britannia stage manager Frederick Wilton lived from 1863 to 1875 was still classified as 'fairly comfortable' on Booth's London poverty maps of 1889. But the area round New North Road had declined from the 1850s when the master of the Wesleyan Day School in Mintern Street marvelled at the expensively dressed female worshippers in New North Road Chapel. Bridport Place had three families to a house by the late 1880s and a local butcher commented that his trade in several joints of meat per family a week had dropped off, as the poor shopped in Pitfield Street for smaller meat pieces.

Some streets were far worse than Bridport Place. Wilmer Gardens, on the east side of Hoxton Street, had been a small lane of cottage-style houses with Ingram's rubber factory at one end. In the 1880s it was redeveloped with tenement houses, and the owner, who later went bankrupt took in tenants that Booth described as 'riff-raff'. Rents were difficult to collect and families large – one mission worker found over 600 children eligible for free meals. In the period before the First World War, A.S. Jasper remembered the blocks as rat-infested, fronted by mud, filth and garbage. Inside the flats stank and the inhabitants could afford little furniture. It was streets like these that housed Booth's criminals – burglars, receivers of stolen goods and street gangs. With high levels of chronic unemployment, what money there was went on sweets for children and drink for adults; one clergyman claimed that half the population of his parish was drunk on Saturday night. But for those that could afford it there were the local theatres, music halls, weddings and funerals, jaunts to Epping Forest and the annual expedition down to Kent to work on the hop farms.

Haggerston was distinctly a little better off than Hoxton, though it also had its population of thieves and its patches of poor streets along the Regent's Canal and round Maidstone Street. Boston Street in Haggerston, where the original St Augustine's

Mission Church was squeezed between a pub and a sausage factory, had two-storey four-roomed houses with a 'tenement' kitchen at the back and an additional tiny room above it. The small backyards had only one tap – whose water might be shared between three or more sets of lodgers. Poor sanitation and overcrowding contributed to the death rate in a cholera outbreak in Haggerston in the summer of 1866 and the more drastic smallpox epidemic in the winter of 1870. But Boston Street did have running water, and there were few basement dwellers in Haggerston, in contrast to some of the courts off Hoxton Street.

Shoreditch Vestry tried to close some of the worst of the houses, but it was left to the voluntary sector to try to help the poor. The growth in Anglican parishes in the nineteenth century had been matched by activity among nonconformists. There were Wesleyan Methodist churches at New North Road (1848) and Hackney Road, with rival Primitive Methodists at Cooper's Gardens, Hackney Road and the United Methodists at Maidstone Street (1852). One of the Maidstone Street lay preachers, James Johnson was a founder of the Lighthouse movement and in 1896 slum clearance in the Goldsmith's Row area gave the congregation the opportunity to rebuild the renamed Harbour Light and Methodist Church (bombed in June 1944).

The earliest Shoreditch Baptists had met in a house in Curtain Road from 1829 and used an adjoining warehouse to run a school for ragged children. They moved to Providence Hall in Worship Street in 1833 and built Providence Chapel on the south side of Hackney Road in 1836. William Cuff became pastor in 1872 and under his ministry a new church, the Shoreditch Tabernacle, replaced the old building in 1879. Cuff was President of the Baptist Union in 1900 and remained minister until 1917. Thereafter the congregation declined, and the tabernacle, badly damaged by bombing was demolished after the war. A post-war revival and a new church, opened in 1963 have ensured the survival of the congregation when many other nonconformist churches failed to survive.

Other religions included the Mormons, active in Haggerston from 1852 to 1862 and a group of Shakers, meeting in a small house in Stanley Road in 1872. Their dancing, shouting and clapping prompted the neighbours, led by the vicar of Holy Trinity Church, to petition Shoreditch Vestry to have the noise stopped.

Anglicans, nonconformists and Catholics alike were all seeking to bring religion to their local communities and all introduced a variety of social and educational services to assist the poorest in their neighbourhoods. St Monica's Catholic Church founded in 1863 served the poor Irish community around Hoxton Square. In St Augustine's parish in Haggerston, the sisters of St Saviour's Priory had provided help during the smallpox epidemic of 1870–1. The ten sisters were aided by Robert Brett and Dr Sutton, Shoreditch's medical officer of health, to establish a temporary hospital in the Hackney Road burial ground; while the sisters provided clothes to replace the infected garments and sent convalescents off to Homes in the country. After the epidemic had subsided the sisters ran their own surgery, with prescription charges at the bare minimum. They also provided halfpenny dinners for children, heathen teas preceding baptism services, free meals for out of work men and the sick, and tickets for bread, groceries and coal. There were crèches to enable women to go back to work, clubs and beds for destitute girls without homes. In 1879 the sisters founded the Mission of the Good Shepherd in an upper room of a workshop in 'Piggy's Island' near Goldsmiths' Row. Here the coster girls were thought to be the toughest in the East End; standing in groups on street corners or outside pubs with their white aprons, white shawls and profusely feathered hats, shouting and screaming at any unrecognised passer-by. The Mission gave them a meeting place, and later a night refuge, while a coffee bar provided cheap meals for factory girls in their short mid-day break and lasted until local authority welfare services were begun after the First World War.

Missionaries also made use of sinful theatres. William Noble hired the Royal Standard Theatre in 1878 to launch his Blue Ribbon Army temperance movement. Casting around for an alternative, he found the former McDonald's Music Hall, Hoxton Hall, which had lost its licence for public performances. In the event it was bought by the Quaker biscuit maker W.I. Palmer in 1879, who made it available to Noble and his Army. The Blue Ribbon movement provided its own label tea and coffee and published a journal. Sarah Rae, wife of the secretary of the movement, founded the Guild of Girls of Good Life in 1885. Initially working with a small group of thirteen to sixteen-year-olds, she soon found that 'experience proved that (this) was a dangerous age for many as they get into all sorts of bad ways through running wild in the streets', so the age limit was reduced to thirteen and below. Despite its motto 'Good wives for working men', Mrs Rae and her helpers offered a wide range of activities, which by 1893 included purchase of cheap underwear and dress-making, elocution and reading classes, a library, drawing and painting, singing, various saving schemes and a cottage at Southend for visits. The wife of the Rector of Shoreditch, Mrs Buss, was an influential member of the governing body, which in 1937 included one countess, one viscountess and nine titled ladies among its twenty-nine members; an aristocratic assembly of the great and good at work.

W.I. Palmer left Hoxton Hall to the Quaker Bedford Institute on his death, but this made little change to the various missionary activities and the need for their social work continued through the 1920s and 30s. The dislocations of the war — bombing and evacuation — disrupted but did not end the work and though in 1943 the Girls' Guild was said to be 'but a shadow of its former buxom self', it survived until 1960. More serious was the decline in religious activity and the turning away from the Sunday school. Slum clearance by Shoreditch Council caused Hoxton Hall gradually to change the emphasis of its activities, and as the 1963 centenary celebrations coincided with the formation of the British Music Hall Society, there was a chance to see what a rare survival Hoxton Hall had become. Theatre became a more important part of the work of the Hall and restoration followed in 1968.

Most notable among the nonconformists was the Hoxton Market Christian Mission. The founders, saddlers John and Lewis Burtt, had themselves been rescued from the streets and educated in a Ragged School. They took children into their basement workshop and offered them shelter, warmth, food and second-hand clothes. With the help of members of Rectory Road Congregational Church in Hackney, the brothers started home visits, and five years after their work had begun, funds allowed them to acquire premises in Hoxton Market in 1886. Religious activity included meetings, a local Band of Hope and bible classes. The Hoxton Market premises were rebuilt in 1904 and further enlarged in 1914. During the First World War the Mission played a strong social role in supporting families whose principal wage earners were in the armed services, and in the hard times of the post-war decades helped with assisted emigration; as well as feeding and clothing children. Replacement boots were a speciality, while the slogan 'Daddy Burtts for dinner' became part of Hoxton folklore. After the death of the last of the Burtt brothers in 1937, a memorial home was opened at Wadhurst in Sussex, moving to Bognor Regis in 1948, giving convalescence space to sick children. In the Second World War the Mission helped to evacuate local disabled people, first to Hastings in East Sussex, then Malvern in Worcestershire, and finally to Heanor in Derbyshire. The Mission premises, gutted in an oil bomb fire on 10 May 1941, were rebuilt and re-opened in 1952. The Mission survived the creation of the welfare state and did not close until the early 1980s.

Other groups included the Costers' Mission, founded in 1861 and linked to the Ragged School Union, which used Costers' Hall as a base for services, concerts, Sunday school, a mutual loan society and various temperance lodges. Soup kitchens played their part in time of hardship for the unemployed and their children; Jackson's soup kitchen was praised after its work in the hard winter of 1902. The work of religious groups was to remain important in the lives of Shoreditch's poor until the formation of the welfare state, but in the twentieth century it was to be supplemented by increased activity from the new Shoreditch Borough Council, the London County Council and voluntary secular agencies.

An artist's impression of the inside of a Shoreditch house, where one room was shared between two families – four adults and seven children. Food was mostly eaten at a fried fish shop, with only beer and tea drunk in the room itself. Drawing by Bryan de Grineau for the *Illustrated London News*, October 1919.

Boston Street, looking south from the junction with Holms Street in 1955, with its four room houses plus extensions at the rear. One side of Boston Street was destroyed in the Blitz; this side had been all but cleared by 1961, with just the shop and the adjoining houses still standing. Today this area is part of Haggerston Park.

Crooked Billet Yard, between Nos. 9–11 Kingsland Road, was entered via an alley under the North London Railway. There had been a pub of that name here before 1770, by which time it had become the Red Lion and the small houses may have been built as early as the 1740s. This group were on the north side of the yard and were photographed in 1933, shortly before demolition.

Caroline Place was a narrow dead-end lane a little to the north of Crooked Billet Yard, and this 1920 view looks west to the back of Shoreditch School. This end of the street was bombed in October 1940 and was cleared after the war, to be incorporated into the school site.

This day nursery was just one of the social services provided by the Anglican St Saviour's Priory and is seen here in 1910.

Claude Eliot Lads' Club premises were at 147 Bridport Place in 1908 when this view was taken, to be included in a benefit concert programme. The club, founded in 1903 by Revd Claude Eliot, vicar of Christ Church, Hoxton in New North Road, moved the following year to a former pub that had lost its licence. Activities included reading, debating, boxing, cricket, football, athletics and a rifle range and the club had its own Lads' Brigade, some of whom are lined up outside.

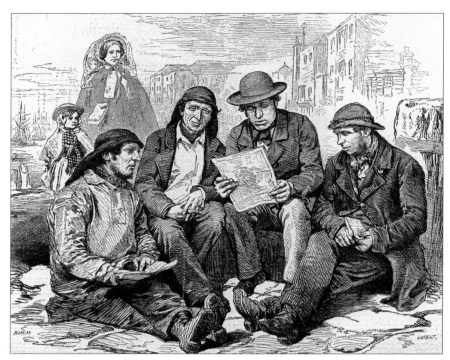

By the mid-1850s Haggerston had a reputation for drunkness and was attracting missionary activity. These four coal heavers, who appeared in the *British Workman* in July 1856, have just been presented with a tract by the lady at the rear. The group included James Skinner of Gloucester Street, who worked at the Independent Gas Works, shifting twenty to thirty tons of coal on his back each day and had a thirst to match. After a drinking bout that left him with 'something like the horrors', he took the pledge and kept to it for over five years.

The north side of Hoxton Square, with St Monica's Catholic Church, 1921.

Two faces of parochial work in the High Church parish of St Augustine's, Haggerston. Above: the parish priest, Father H.A. Wilson catches some of his flock outside Alfred Godfrey's off-licence, 24 Yorkton Street, in the spring of 1942. The window is taped up against bomb blast. Wilson, the author of *Death over Haggerston*, included many anecdotes of wartime life in his parish, including the man who surveyed the remains of his back yard and commented: 'That old hen of mine is a marvel: they blew her hutch to bits last night and she laid an egg this morning: *that's* what I call business as usual.' Below: a dance in progress at the parish hall in the 1920s.

An open-air service outside Hoxton Hall, Hoxton Street, about 1906.

Chidren line up outside Hoxton Market Christian Mission about 1900. The Mission premises, just visible on the right hand side, were completely rebuilt in 1904.

# 8. ENTERTAINMENT

Hoxton had been a thriving resort in the sixteenth century, with taverns, pleasure grounds like Pimlico and bowling greens. Among the historic inns, The Old Blue Last, claiming to date from 1700, was the first pub to sell the newly brewed porter, supplied from the Bell Brewhouse in Shoreditch in 1722. The old house was rebuilt when Great Eastern Street was constructed in 1876. For the more or less sober there might be the prospect of a dip in Perillous Pool, on the western edge of the later City Road, so called, as the sixteenth century historian John Stow succinctly remarked, because 'divers youths swimming there have been drowned'. So dangerous did it become, that it was closed for some years, then, in 1743 William Kemp took a sixty-four year lease from the landowners, St Bartholomew's Hospital, built two houses alongside, and turned it into a splendid swimming pool and fishpond. With an eye for publicity, Kemp renamed his development Peerless Pool, and even had the adjoining road renamed from Pest House Row (with its unwelcome associations of the plague) to Bath Street. Peerless Pool lasted until 1807, when the lease ran out and most of the site was built over, though an open-air swimming pool survived until 1869.

Shepherdess Walk was originally no more than a field path from the City to Islington, and a tavern established there by the mid-eighteenth century, the Shepherd and Shepherdess, offered frumenty, cakes and cream in its pleasure garden. The construction of the City Road in 1761 increased trade. The garden was still doing business in the Napoleonic period, but the adjoining area was rapidly being developed after 1815. One of the principal contractors was the builder Thomas Rouse, who is said to have acquired the Shepherd and Shepherdess as a tavern for his work-force. Rouse's neighbour was Dodd the Dustman, whose dustheaps adjoined the sides of the Regent's Canal at the top end of Shepherdess Walk, and who served as the model for Dickens' Noddy Boffin in *Our Mutual Friend*. By 1821 Rouse had rebuilt his tavern, naming it The Eagle and put on a wide range of shows including wrestling matches and balloon ascents.

And there were concerts. Begining with Harmonic Meetings at which professional musicians entertained workers, by the autumn of 1831 the regular public concerts were accompanied by an organ and a self-playing piano and finished with fireworks. Rouse

The Eagle Tavern from City Road, from a drawing by J. Shury, 1841.

had acquired a Gothic entrance, said to have come from the coronation of William IV at Westminster Abbey, joined in the summer of 1832 by a Chinese pavilion in the grounds to cater for the increasing audiences. Mythological figures decorated the walls, there was a grand doorway from the recently demolished Wanstead House in Essex, and a peal of invisible bells was added to the pinnacle over the entrance.

To match this splendour the gardens were given a new name – the Royal Eagle Coronation Pleasure Grounds, with the Grecian Saloon, a rotunda seating up to 700 people. Later additions included an aviary and a dancing platform and such was the fame of the new establishment that the violinist Niccolo Paganini visited in August 1832. By the mid-1830s evening concerts were held in the Grecian Saloon. An overture, and a sung chorus would be followed by musical farce; the whole evening always being presided over by Rouse himself from his armchair, nicknamed 'Bravo' Rouse, from the cheers that greeted him at the end of the performance. Dickens visited the grounds in 1836 and wrote up his experiences in *Sketches by Boz*. Miss J'mima Ivins and her companions pass the gate and once inside find 'walks, beautifully gravelled and planted – and the refreshment boxes, painted and ornamented like so

The entrance to the Grecian Saloon, an engraving of about 1835.

many snuff boxes – and the variegated lamps shedding their rich light upon the company's heads – and the Moorish band playing at one end of the gardens and an opposition military band playing at the other. Then the waiters were rushing to and fro with glasses of negus and glasses of brandy and water and bottles of ale . . . As to the concert room, there was never anything so splendid. There was an orchestra for the singers, all paint, gilding and plate glass . . . the audience were seated on elevated benches round the room and crowded into every part of it and everybody was eating and drinking as comfortably as possible.' After the concert the audience could promenade in the gardens, though Dickens had J'mima Ivins and her friend's male companions come to blows with two other men, a reminder that Rouse's audience was a noisy and rough one. Smoking and drinking went on during performances of all kinds, and if the show was not felt to be good enough then oranges and pork pies would be thrown with vigour.

Rouse experimented in other ways. It is likely that he introduced the term 'vaudeville' to England, imported from France, where it was used to describe musical shows with satirical and topical themes. Rouse also attracted performers with considerable talent, including the singers Sims Reeves and Frederick Robson. Profits were sufficient for Rouse to pull down the original tavern he had built and replace it with a palatial new Eagle, which was to last until 1901. In the following year he opened a new pavilion in the grounds, the Olympic Temple, used for ballet and opera. Some performances lost money, but in one year an estimated deficit of £2,000 on the theatre was more than made up by a profit of £5,000 on the tavern; while benefit performances from 1841 onwards ensured that money went to charities. The free spending that went on may have lead to the adaption of an old Morris dance tune to new words:

> Up and down the City Road
> In and out the Eagle,
> That's the way the money goes,
> Pop goes the Weasel

Supposedly it was tailors pawning their flat-irons (weasels) for drink money that led to the mysterious last line of the rhyme. Rouse finally retired in 1841, handing over to the progenitor of a theatrical dynasty, Benjamin Conquest.

Benjamin Oliver – the name Conquest was assumed for the stage – had moved from being a poor actor to one of the lessees of the Garrick Theatre in Whitechapel from 1830 and had prospered until it was destroyed by fire in 1846. With experience of comic acting gained at the Garrick, at other London venues and on tour, Benjamin soon moved from opera and classical plays to pantomime, and it was these annual extravagances that made the Conquest name famous. Benjamin's son George was a natural acrobat and a gifted author, populating his creations with weird creatures – apes, giant spiders and crabs; even an octopus. Benjamin died in 1872, but George and the Conquest family kept the lease up until 1878, when they sold up and moved to the Surrey Theatre, south of the Thames.

The new lessee was T.G. Clark, who kept on the Conquest company, and continued in the pantomime tradition, but his expertise was in marine stores, not in the theatre. In June 1881 he sold the Grecian at auction and the successful bidder was none other than General William Booth, who was looking for new headquarters for the Salvation Army. Booth proposed to banish the play actors, their immoral audience and the 'demon drink', but was brought up against the terms of Rouse's original lease to Benjamin Oliver, which insisted that the Eagle Tavern must be used as a public house. Booth evaded this by retaining the licence, but refusing to sell alcohol. There was trouble with a rowdy local crowd, and also with Shoreditch

Sketches of *The Grim Goblin*, a Grecian production of 1876. George Conquest played a gigantic ape and the octopus, whose machinery enabled him to mimic the movements of the real thing.

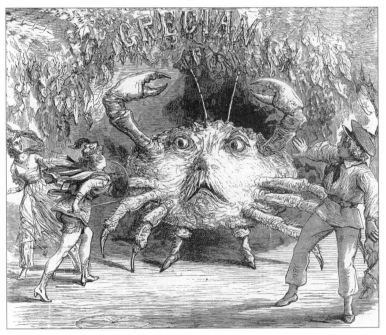

A scene from *Spitze Spitze the Spider Crab or the Sprite of Spitzebergen* also from the 1876 season, in which the stage was made to resemble an aquarium and George supposedly playing a crab 'with dark spots on the carapace that gradually transformed themselves into flaming eyes'. In fact the crab was a puppet fitted over a five-year-old child wearing a false head of Conquest, and with movement controlled by strings from above.

AND NOW THAT YOU HAVE COLLECTED ALL THIS MONEY, MR. BOOTH, WHAT
DO YOU INTEND TO DO WITH IT?

A cartoon from *The Entr'Acte Annual* of 1883 looking back on the efforts General Booth had made to fund-raise the previous year, when he was able to use the money to buy the Eagle Tavern and Grecian Theatre.

The grounds of the Eagle, showing the Chinese Pavilion, with demolition in progress. A watercolour by J.P. Emslie, 1899.

Vestry when Booth submitted his bill for police protection to them. In the end the former London Orphan Asylum at Clapton proved more attractive and the Salvationists left in 1884, allowing the Grecian to become a music hall. A year later the fifteen-year-old Matilda Wood made her first apperance on stage here – the beginning of the career of music hall star Marie Lloyd. At the end of the Army's lease in 1898, the site was sold and the grounds cleared. The Eagle Tavern also went, replaced by a modern and smaller successor, which still retains the old eagle on its top pinnacle.

There were other public houses that used the stage to boost the sale of drink, adding or extending a room at the rear to hold it and some scenery, and calling the result a saloon. Among those that did so in the late 1830s were the Union Saloon and the Britannia public house. The latter had been in existence in 1792, with its own gardens. Many saloons were short-lived, like the Albert, at 106 Shepherdess Walk, which lasted only from 1843 to 1851, but others were to go on to greatness, and it was in the 1840s that agitation brought about changes in the licensing laws that benefited the saloons. Under the theatre acts only the licensed West End theatres were allowed to put on Shakespeare, but the saloons could provide what was mainly music hall style entertainment with some drama – often very mutilated – thrown in. In 1839 the licensee of the Union Saloon was Samuel Lane, a Devon man, who provided two performances a week of music, singing and drama, the latter being more than he was licensed for. In September 1839, the Union Saloon was raided. There were about 900 in the audience in a room about 60 ft long, with the actors performing on a tiny stage only 7 ft high and 17 ft wide and panic ensued as people escaped over the roof. Three gallons of beer were spilt in the raid and Lane's wife, who was underneath them was arrested in her soaked clothes and not allowed to change. The resulting prosecution and fines closed down the Union, though the charge of performing unlicensed drama was thrown out.

Lane now moved to the Britannia, which already had a music and dancing licence, also had a rough reputation: there had been a fatal fight outside in 1839. Hoxton's fields were being rapidly built over in the 1830s. The new residents wanted local entertainment but if Lane was to keep his licence, he had to convince the magistrates that he was not running a disreputable house, even though his audience might include thieves, burglars and prostitutes. Lane took the risk and built a theatre in the grounds of the tavern, but after a briefly successful season, he lost the licence and it was not until the Theatre Regulation Act of 1843, which removed the power to licence from local magistrates and placed it with the Lord Chamberlain's office, that the future of the Britannia and other local theatres was secured. The Britannia, the Eagle and the Grecian and other houses were licensed at last, though in future drinking and smoking inside the saloons were prohibited. Lane was still to have trouble with the police, who accused

MESSRS. BIGWOOD AND REYNOLDS.

G.B. Bigwood and Joseph Reynolds, two of the 'Brit's' long-serving actors. From *The Entr'Acte* of 1886.

him of attracting prostitutes, thieves and 'blackguard boys who crowded about the front of the saloon for the purpose of selling Tickets of Admission to the Passers by – insulting those who would not be purchasers – using obscene language and being otherwise most disorderly', but he was able to rebut the charges. After re-opening, the Britannia Saloon had its own local company and dramatists, and put on popular melodramas again. On the death of his first wife, Samuel married Sarah Borrow, who, as Sara Wilton, had been one of his principal actresses.

Dickens was a member of the audience in 1850 and was impressed by the comparative sobriety and the youth of the audience, many hardly out of their teens. Food was in abundance: 'Huge ham sandwiches, piled on trays like deals in a timber yard, were handed around for the hungry and there was no stint of oranges, cakes, brandy-balls or similar refreshments.' In 1858 Sam decided to demolish the old saloon. The building regulations in force at the time of its construction had not been exactly strict, and the author John Hollingshead recalled boring holes at the stage end with cricket stumps, letting out the scent of the footlights 'that indescribable bouquet of stale gas, orange peel, damp playbills and mouldy scenery', and allowing the words of the play in performance to be heard. The new building, designed by architects

Finch, Hill and Praire, was to have much greater audience capacity and enable Sam to put on serious plays. He was able to argue for a change of title, and when the new building opened in November 1858, it was as the Britannia Theatre. The tavern remained at the front, but there were seats for 3,250 people, good fire exits and fine brickwork, left uncovered in places. The house was painted salmon pink, enriched with fawn, white and gold and lit by cut glass chandeliers. There were refreshment rooms for each of the three classes of seats. When Dickens returned in 1860, he found much to praise – clean air, carpets – and his piece was reprinted by the 'Brit' as a supporting puff.

The new theatre quickly settled into a yearly cycle; pantomime for the first twelve weeks, followed by a melodrama, with one night for Sara Lane's benefit, then a change of programme at Easter with a burlesque or another melodrama. Sam and Sara Lane would be away in the summer and visiting artists would fill in, before Sara returned to star in an autumn melodrama, and an annual performance of *Guy Fawkes*, with fireworks. The season finished with a special 'festival' with all the company in their favourite roles and floral tributes from the audience to Sara. After Sam's death in 1872, Sara assumed the management, and continued to act, performing regularly as the principal boy well into old age. The Lane company drew on its own dramatists, notably Colin Hazelwood and Dibden Pitt, and resident comedians, George Bigwood and Edward Elton. Later stars in the 1880s included the Lupinos and Marie Lloyd. The theatre also employed its own carpenters, musicians, scenic artists, and many others. Some specialists went on to other careers – William Batey, the caterer, who founded a noted lemonade and ginger beer factory just off the Kingsland Road around 1853 and William Pain, the pyrotechnist, who may have been a relative of the founder of Pain's Fireworks. The period of unchanged management encouraged long associations of individuals and families, but also kept the theatre in close touch with the bulk of its audience. There were always West End visitors, and these included George Bernard Shaw, in his capacity as theatre critic for the *Saturday Review* in 1898, but it was the local people who kept up the profits.

Gradually, though there were changes. Hoxton was becoming a poorer neighbourhood at the end of the century. Sara Lane had a stroke and died in 1899; her funeral procession, behind a six horse glass-panelled carriage, a floral carriage and six mourning coaches brought out so many people that Hoxton Street was blocked. But the 'Queen' of Hoxton left behind her a theatre that had aged and was now becoming unsafe. An LCC inspection compelled her nephews, the Craufords to carry out repairs. In the event the rising expenses proved too much, and in 1904 they leased it to others. Variety was tried, but with little success, and in the period 1909 to 1913 it was used for boxing, a brief theatrical revival under George Conquest, and then became a cinema. Badly damaged in the blitz of 1941, the remains were cleared after the war; a sad end to a great theatre.

The scene from the stage of the newly rebuilt Britannia Theatre in 1858. Charles Dickens was impressed: 'Magnificently lighted by a firmament of sparkling chandeliers, the building was ventilated to perfection. My sense of smell, without being particularly delicate, has been so offended in some commoner places of resort, that I have been obliged to leave. The air of this theatre was fresh, cool and wholesome. It has been constructed from the ground to the roof with a careful reference to sight and sound in every corner, the result is that its form is beautiful, and that the appearance of the audience, as seen from the proscenium, with every face in it commanding the stage, and the whole is so admirably raked and turned to that centre, and is highly remarkable in its union of vastness with compactness. The stage itself and all its appurtenances of machinery, cellarage, height and breadth, are on a scale more like the Scala at Milan, or the Grand Opera at Paris than any notion a stranger would be likely to form of the Britannia Theatre at Hoxton, a mile north of St. Luke's Hospital in the Old Street Road. "The Forty Thieves" might be played here, and every thief ride his real horse; and the disguised captain bring in his oil jars on a train of real camels and nobody would be put out of the way.'

Characters from *King Do Dah*, a Britannia pantomime of 1900.

The Britannia Theatre and the view north up Hoxton Street, about 1936. By this time the 'Brit' had ceased to put on live productions and was used as a cinema.

All that remained of the former City of London Theatre in Norton Folgate in 1909; the back had been demolished in 1872.

The Varieties Theatre at 18–20 Pitfield Street opened as a competitor to the Britannia in 1867. After a poor start it was taken over by George Harwood, the manager of the St Leonard's Hall penny gaff. The Varieties was a rough introduction for many artists, including Dan Leno and the Great Macdermott, who made his reputation singing *We don't want to Fight, but by Jingo if we do*, which added a new word to the English language. Unpopular acts were on the receiving end of a another kind of variety – rotten fruit. Nor were the actors always well behaved, one real life fight ended up on stage, to hearty cheers. After 1901 the manager, Leonard Mortimer, also organised benefits to provide dinners and free holidays for local children. Changing fashions brought a conversion to the cinema in 1923; after closure the theatre was put to industrial use and was demolished in 1980.

MR. JOHN DOUGLASS.

John Douglass junior, playwright and manager of the Standard Theatre. A cartoon from *The Entr'Acte Annual*, 1883.

Shoreditch had two other theatres closer to the boundary with the City. The City of London Theatre on the west side of Norton Folgate, had been built in 1834, designed by Samuel Beazley, although financial problems delayed its opening until 1837, when it was described as 'the handsomest house in London'. It had a stage 30 ft wide and 38 ft deep and could seat over 1,000. Its first productions included a dramatisation of Dickens' new book, *The Pickwick Papers*. It should have benefited from the opening of the nearby Eastern Counties railway station in 1840, but a succession of short-lived licensees had a problem in gauging what could pull in the crowds; an ambitious performance of Sheridan's *School for Scandal* in 1844 was not what was wanted. Successful actress and beauty of her day, Mrs Honey could succeed on the boards, but she too failed as a manager. However in 1848, manager Nelson Lee took the lease and succeeded with pantomimes, and serious drama, mostly taken on from West End productions that had enjoyed a good run. In the late 1850s he found, like many another after him, that crime productions pay. Lee retired in 1865 and thereafter new licensees failed to maintain a winning formula. John Douglass used the theatre for a year in 1866 after his own theatre, the Standard, had been burnt out, but the decline was not stopped and when the Standard re-opened in 1867, the competition proved too much. Not even a Lee pantomime or a circus could save the City, and Lee sold it to the Great Eastern Railway in 1868. After a period as a music hall, charging prices so low that it was competing with the cheapest of all entertainments, the penny gaffs, it became a soup kitchen and a temperance hall, before being destroyed by fire in 1871.

The Standard Theatre at 203–4 Shoreditch High Street, began as a small converted shop in 1835, seating around 400. For two years, manager John Gibson operated without a licence of any kind. In 1845 there was a fire and the Standard was refronted and gas lit. Gibson produced a wide range of melodrama, ballet, and Shakespeare (with songs). In 1844 Nelson Lee and a partner took over, and introduced pantomimes and equestrian performances, using tracking to replace the stage with a ring. John Douglass became the manager in 1848, mixing Shakespeare and serious drama with pantomime and opera. Disaster struck in 1866 after a production of the Weber opera *Der Freischutz*, when fire engulfed the theatre. The East London Water Company, 'with a deep-seated love of pelf' limited the water supply on Sundays and the theatre and all its properties, except a comedian's wig, were destroyed.

Douglass was determined to rebuild, and the new theatre which opened in December 1867 was vast, claiming to be 'The Largest and Most Magnificent Theatre in the World'. The first pantomime production included over a hundred dancers in the ballet scene, but Douglass' extravagance paid off, attracting audiences of 50,000 in a week, and he was able to bring in West End companies, with stars like Henry Irving.

Douglass died in 1879, but his family continued his successes, using special effects like the large tank used in sea scenes. Before the tank, more primitive methods had to be used. In one production a ship built on rockers was supposed to sink through a painted cloth, supported by numerous small boys waving their arms and hopping to imitate a stormy sea. One night the boys asked for a pay rise from 6d to a shilling, which was refused. On the following night, just as the ship was about to sink, a boy's face appeared from beneath the sheet and shouted to the stage-manager, 'Hi Mister, what about it ? Are you having sixpenny or shilling waves tonight?' 'Sixpenny ones, you young scoundrel', roared the stage manager. Industrial action ensued, and the ship sank in a dead calm. But the stage manager caught up with the ringleader after the performance, and thrashed him, after which every show was accompanied by a rough sea and very angry waves – at 6d only. The play *Daybreak* included a Derby scene with real horses dashing through the theatre and out onto Holywell Lane. An obliging policeman stopped the traffic each night and took part in the betting on who would win! Financial difficulties brought the Douglass era to an end in 1892. The Melville family took over, rebuilding the theatre entirely in 1897 and producing popular melodramas, but could not compete with the newly established local cinemas and they sold out in 1911. Thereafter the Standard became a variety theatre, and then Shoreditch

Nelson Lee's period included some curious productions. *What is It?* featured Senior Hervio Nano, alias Harvey Leach, an American monkey impersonator, who posed as the Missing Link. Leach died of his exertions in Shoreditch in 1847.

The Standard Theatre and adjoining houses in Shoreditch High Street in 1879.

At the turn of the century the Melvilles turned to a series of dramas based on contemporary images of the temptations and weaknesses of women. *A Girl's Crossroads* was one of them and for a while they drew in the audiences.

The interior of St Leonard's Hall, in 1856, situated in 'the neighbourhood of old clothes, fried fish, baked potatos and cheap theatricals' as the magazine *Paul Pry* put it. Each evening included three panoramas, with duets and comic singing.

Olympia cinema in 1926. It was pulled down for rebuilding in 1939, but construction was halted by the outbreak of war and never resumed.

For those that could not afford a proper theatre there were the 'penny gaffs'; the bottom end of the market, where for a penny, an often juvenile audience squeezed into a tiny shop, illuminated with candles to see Shakespeare reduced to twenty minutes or a blood-curdling drama. Gaffs first appeared in the 1830s and were at their height in the 1850s and 60s. There were two in the vicinity of Shoreditch High Street – St Leonard's Hall at No. 153 from 1854–70 and Bianchi's at 118 Holywell Lane from 1854–66. Passers-by could be tempted in by suggestive advertising, and shows that had more in common with grotesque circus acts. In 1887 police raided 166 Shoreditch High Street, where 'the tallest soldier in the world' and two fat women were on display 'and John Paul, a man of colour' shouted at the door to attract custom and played the barrel organ. A prosecution ensued for keeping a 'disorderly house'. A cut above the gaffs were the music halls. The Eastern Alhambra at 202 Shoreditch High Street seems to

Benjamin Pollock with a toy theatre and character sheets in his shop, 73 Hoxton Street, 1929.

have been an outlet for a ginger beer maker to sell more of his wares; it never aspired to the heights of a licence and lasted only from 1867 to 1875. McDonald's at 64b Hoxton Street had the briefest of careers. It was built by James Mortimer, a builder of model dwellings for the poor, in 1863 and its shows included musicals and performing dogs. Competition from the newly opened Varieties Theatre in Pitfield Street and a loss of licence lead to closure and sale in 1879, when it was taken over as a Quaker meeting hall. In 1963 a centenary music hall performance was given there, and this was the origin of the revived Hoxton Hall, the last in a long line of Shoreditch theatres and halls.

The stage-struck had another place of refuge in Hoxton. By 1851 printer John Redington was established at 208 Hoxton Old Town (later 73 Hoxton Street), selling, among other wares, plays and sheets for toy theatres. After his death in 1876, his son-in-law Benjamin Pollock carried on the business, issuing splendid large-sized scenes. Among his customers was Robert Louis Stevenson, who had owned a toy theatre as a boy. His article *Penny Plain and Twopence Coloured*, published in 1884, came out at a time when the original sheets had ceased to be printed, but it brought a revival and successful publicity so that Pollock was able to carry on until his death in 1937. Although the shop

Cover of the score for Gainsborough Studio's
period drama, *The Wicked Lady*, 1946.

was bombed in the Second World War, the business was purchased and revived and today Pollock's Toy Theatres trade from Scala Street, keeping alive a passion that went back to the beginning of the nineteenth century.

Shoreditch had played its part in the history of English theatre, and it was also to contribute to the history of the cinema. In 1919 the American Players Lasky Film Company took over the former Metropolitan Railway generating station in Poole Street. They carried out the necessary adaptions, but could not make successful films, and in 1924 the studios were taken over by a British company who became Gainsborough Pictures. Early successes starred Ivor Novello; later stars included the Crazy Gang, Will Hay and Arthur Askey, but perhaps the best loved of the Gainsborough pictures were *Oh, Mr Porter!*, with Will Hay, and Alfred Hitchcock's *The Lady Vanishes* of 1938. In 1939, fears that an air raid would cause the exceptionally high chimney to fall on the studio, closed the place for a while, but the Gainsborough company were soon back in residence, making period costume drama. Final closure came in 1949, and for many years the former studios were a carpet warehouse. In 1996 planning permission is being sought to demolish the buildings, with only a small display set to remain on the site to recall Shoreditch's past celluloid glories.

The east side of Shoreditch High Street, showing Nos. 91–8 in April 1875; respectively Henry Casey, tailor at 91, John Todd, milliner at 92, Alfred Stedall's mantle warehouse, David Allen glass dealer at 94, Philip Cohen, 'feather manufacturer' at 95, George Wilson, confectioner at 96, George Hawker, baker at 97 and John Jones, tripe dresser at 98. At this stage the High Street was still a real shopping street, with buildings from the seventeenth and early eighteenth century behind plaster and weatherboard facades.

Dawson's drapery shop, on the corner of East and City Roads in 1902; a watercolour by Charles Ivanhoe. The horse tram gave way to an electric successor in July 1907.

# 9. BUSINESS & INDUSTRY

The earliest industrial activity in Shoreditch seems to have been the mills; windmills were shown on early engravings in the vicinity of Balmes House, and there was an oatmeal mill at the south-east end of Kingsland Road, south of Cotton's Gardens from the early 1580s, which survived to the middle of the eighteenth century. Indeed there were a variety of industries in the Chassereau map of 1745. The fields of Hoxton and Haggerston were already being worked for brick earth and this was to continue until development was completed in the 1830s. There was an extensive tile works just north of Hackney Road, with a warehouse on the line of the later Tuilerie Street. Open ground to the south of Holywell Lane, on the borders of Moorfield and to the west of the Hackney Road burial ground were set out as tenter grounds; for the stretching and drying of cloth. There were two extensive vinegar factories. Wittenoom's, east of Paul Street, founded prior to 1720, gave way to residential development, but Calvert's, later Champion's, at the junction of Old Street and City Road, was to survive until the late nineteenth century. Francis Smith had run a white lead and colour factory at the Curtain (near the present Hewitt Street) up until 1763, when he was declared bankrupt, and his works were destroyed by arson.

Shoreditch High Street was the principal shopping street by the late eighteenth century, but it also attracted a number of manufacturing businesses. With changes in residential patterns during the nineteenth century, businesses that catered for the domestic market in South Shoreditch were gradually replaced by specialist concerns and wholesalers. North of Old Street, factories had been set up on new sites overlooking fields, or adjoining the Regent's Canal, completed in 1819. These included two of Shoreditch's three gas works. As building development proceeded space for factories to expand was curtailed and factories producing candles, soap, rubber goods and cotton in the 1860s had all been displaced by the 1890s; either ceasing to trade or moving further out to Hackney or beyond. Large industrial sites were also convenient for re-use in the increasing municipal activity from the turn of the nineteenth century: Champion's vinegar works was replaced by local authority flats, and Lawrence Brothers City Iron Works on Pitfield Street made way for the baths, public library and electricity generating station.

The two principal trades associated with Shoreditch are the manufacture of furniture and boots and shoes. The main area of the London furniture making trade in the eighteenth century had been concentrated between St Paul's Churchyard and Aldersgate Street, though as early as 1798 one chair-maker was advertising from addresses in City Road and near Old Street: by 1809 there were a number of timber yards in the Old Street vicinity. The completion of the East and West India Docks and the Regent's Canal saw the establishment of timber yards and saw mills. In turn some furniture makers moved closer to their source of raw material. One of the largest mills, the Eagle Saw Mills alongside Wenlock Basin even provided a generic name for the small streets to the south. But in the main it was new small firms that were established in the area, making cheaper types of furniture. Often employing less than five people, these worked as subcontractors to larger establishments. In addition there were many self-employed men, often working from their own homes, using their own children as labour. Known as garret-masters, from the room or garret they lived in, these men would have just enough credit to buy materials for one or two pieces, which they would then have to hawk round on a barrow from one warehouse to another until they were sold.

By the late 1840s there were substantial divisions in the trade, between those producing quality work and with the protection of a union, mostly working in the West End, and the rest of the trade. Mechanisation of sawmills through steam power had thrown many sawyers out of work, while increasing the ease with which veneer could be produced. The hard bargains driven by speculative builders forced carpenters' wages down, while the increasing numbers of small sweat shops and garret-masters had the same effect on the furniture workers. In his letters to the *Morning Chronicle* in 1849 to 1850, Henry Mayhew described the conditions that East End furniture makers lived under: 'The East-end cabinet-maker's room has one piece of furniture, which is generally the principal, the workman's bench. The walls are bare, and sometimes the half-black plaster is crumbling from them; all is dark and dingy, and of the furniture there is very little, and that, it must be borne in mind, when the occupant is a furniture-maker.'

In contrast were the specialist firms and the wholesalers. Originally these had been concentrated in or near Liverpool Street, but rising rents began an exodus that was completed by the clearance of much of this area for the new stations in the 1860s, making Curtain Road the centre of the East End trade. What seems to have remained behind was the second-hand trade – in 1861 journalist and actor-manager John Hollingshead (born in Hoxton in 1827), described Long Alley as 'that melancholy avenue of vermin-haunted furniture'. Among the wholesalers were associated specialist firms, like W.A. Hudson, who made ironmongery for cabinets, W. Bailey, wholesaler and maker of looking-glasses, and A. Oakden & Sons, hardware factors. These and other firms gradually rebuilt the late Georgian houses of Curtain Road and its environs with 'ebullient late Victorian warehouses'. By the mid-1920s the showrooms of Alfred Goslett & Co. in Tabernacle Street contained more than twenty-five separate showrooms and an entrance hall set out in mock Tudor style, complete with sample reproduction furniture to entice the client sent on directly by retail shops.

After 1920 production was further cheapened by the introduction of plywood and gradually manufacturing firms moved out of Shoreditch to sites in the Lea Valley. James Latham were part of this trend; established in an existing timber yard in Curtain Road by 1851, they acquired premises at Bow, and later, in 1911, another site just north of Lea Bridge, expanding this in 1937, so that when their lease on the Curtain Road site expired in 1940, they moved from Shoreditch altogether.

The local boot and shoe trade had included one or two large firms, like John Carter & Sons, founded in the 1840s, and who built an extensive range of factory buildings on the east side of Kingsland Road, and smaller makers. Mayhew found that in the late 1840s the trade was divided between men's and women's shoe makers; and that industrial disputes had divided the West End trade from the City and East End. Carter's went bankrupt in the 1970s but there is still a Shoreditch shoe trade today.

There was more than one kind of wholesaler attracted by the Shoreditch area. Jeremiah Rotherham began as a draper, but expanded from retail to wholesale, stocking a wide range of haberdashery and other goods in a range of buildings on the east side of Shoreditch High Street; covering over old courts and extinguishing narrow alleys like Hare Alley. Rotherham's were bombed in the Second World War, but another firm survived. Nicholls and Clarke, founded by Samuel Nicholls in 1875, began with glass, but rapidly expanded into sanitary ware, ironmongery, paint and wallpapers.

Shoreditch also played an important part in the tobacco industry. By 1850, forty per cent of London's factories were in Shoreditch and the East End; producing tobacco, cigarettes, cigars and snuff. One of the oldest was R. & J. Hill, established at 175 Shoreditch High Street in 1775, who secured the Admiralty contract for tobacco supplies to the Royal Navy in 1907 and continued through the Second World War, despite the loss of the Shoreditch High Street premises to bombing in May 1941. J.R. Freeman, established in 1838 in Tabernacle Street, making cigars and later cigarettes, moved to the north end of St John's Road (later Pitfield Street). Each of their representatives travelled by train with a huge chest of loose cigar samples, which must have required considerable effort, and were probably greatly relieved when Freeman's became an early convert to the use of the new motor cars before the First World War.

Shoreditch's first local newspaper was the *Shoreditch Observer*, founded in 1857, whose first editor, Enoch Walker, a member of the Shoreditch Vestry, went on to be the principal vestry officer; the clerk from 1870 until his death in 1890. Merged with the *Hackney Express*, the *Observer* kept a keen eye on local affairs until 1915. The *Hackney Gazette*, founded in 1864, and supporting the Liberal party in the nineteenth century, also reported Shoreditch affairs, moving south of the Regent's Canal to its present Kingsland Road offices in 1958.

Shoreditch's first planned market was proposed by Antony Ball and John Brown, who had obtained a long lease of what is now Hoxton Market in 1683/4 and a licence for a bi-weekly food market in 1687/8 but nothing came of the project and in the end it was developed for residential use. By 1843 Shoreditch High Street had its own lively Saturday night market, each stall owner shouting the value of his wares, augmented by the chants of ballad singers, the drunken clamour at the doors of the gin shops and lit by lights from the stalls and the glare of gas lights from the adjoining shops. Vegetables and shell fish were the principal commodities, interspersed with household goods and some cheap toys. By the 1890s it had become a daily market, although the evening remained the busiest time, with custom from those going home from the City and visitors to the local theatres. Book stalls had become a feature of the market and were to remain so until road widening from 1926 onwards brought about closure.

From the 1850s other informal street markets grew up. Hoxton Street's market began around 1850, and forty years later was confined to the area between Fanshaw and Hemsworth Streets. It was a daily market with over two hundred stalls offering fruit, vegetables, clothes, ironmongery, pots, toys and plants. Some stalls were extensions of shops, and had their own awnings and gas lights; the fish and vegetable sellers did the best business. There were smaller street markets in Nile Street (from about 1860), Pitfield Street (from 1850), and Shepherdess Walk (from the 1860s), with Broadway Market in Hackney serving Haggerston. There was little control on what was sold or who could trade and it was not until the twentieth century that licensing was introduced. By the mid-1920s Shoreditch Council provided municipal stalls; the only London borough to do so.

Shoreditch also had its own specialist Sunday morning bird and pet market in Sclater Street. Montagu Williams, a magistrate, visited it in the late 1880s and picked his way down the narrow street, with one side 'entirely taken up with shops, in the windows of which are to be seen all manner of wicker and fancy cages . . . and birds of every description, linnets, mules, canaries, chaffinches, bullfinches, starlings and "furriners"'. The market was known all over London in an era when birds were pitted against one another in singing competitions and accompanying bets. Technically the trade was illegal, but Williams, a self-confessed bird fancier himself, did not support an attempted prosecution brought by Shoreditch Vestry in 1889.

Champion's Vinegar Yard, 1850. A splendidly detailed watercolour, possibly painted from the vantage point of the roof of St Luke's Hospital. City Road and the horse buses are below and Old Street runs off in front, with St Mark's Church beyond the manager's house. In the left background are the crowded houses of Hoxton. Champion's factory closed around the end of the century and the site became the second housing scheme of the Sutton Dwellings Trust in 1913.

The former tile kiln warehouse in Tuilerie Street, seen in 1972. Dating from the late eighteenth century, the tile making site was one of the many business ventures of the Rhodes family in the early nineteenth century. The warehouse was demolished about four years later.

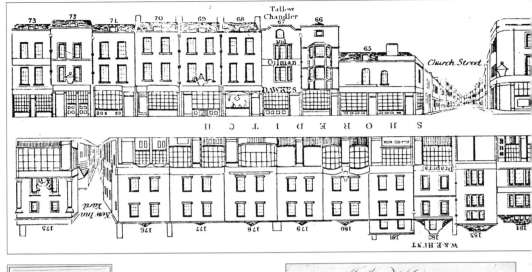

Early nineteenth century trade cards from a ribbon maker and a cabinet maker.

Extracts from Thomas Tallis' views of Shoreditch High Street dating from 1838, taken from drawings by Charles Bigot, one of a number of principal streets published in Tallis's *London Street Views*.

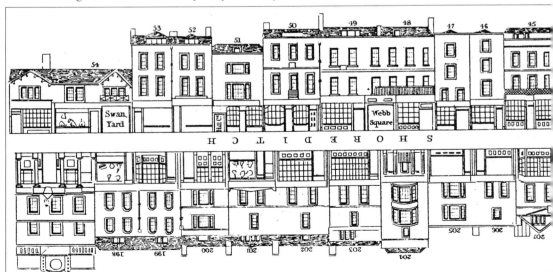

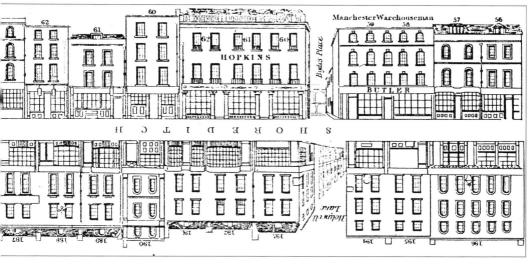

Early nineteenth century trade cards
from a pewterer and a coachmaker.

Curtain Road, looking north from the junction with Great Eastern Street about 1900. The distinctive barrows were used to move furniture from local makers to the display rooms of the main factors.

Furniture making at Beresford and Hick's factory at 131–9 Curtain Road in 1951. The firm had been founded at the beginning of the twentieth century.

Alfred Goslett's showrooms in Tabernacle Street, around 1910, from their trade catalogue. The top view shows the exterior, which included twenty-five separate showrooms. The lower view shows the entrance hall, used for reproduction furniture. Here the furniture retailer could talk to salesmen or bring his own clients to choose for themselves.

Nicholls and Clarke's showroom, 6–8 Shoreditch High Street in 1895. Founded in 1875 by Samuel Nicholls, the business became a limited company in 1890, noted for glass, sanitary fittings and paint, expanding into own brand manufacture in this century. It is still trading today.

One of the more luxurious items from the 1895 catalogue was this patent spray bath, with a copper canopy and mahogany or walnut casing. The tiles at the back were hand-painted.

R. & J. Hill's tobacco factory at 175–7
Shoreditch High Street, around the turn of the
century. This site was destroyed in the Blitz.

Women formed a high proportion of the workforce. This view shows the packing department.

Dotteridge Bros. undertaker's business was founded in 1835 by Samuel
Dotteridge, a Hoxton builder who began arranging funerals as a sideline. This
view and the one opposite show two corners of the carriage yard in Dorset Mews
about 1870. Carriages are being cleaned, and horses fed and watered. Missing
from these views is the distinctive dovecote in the middle of the yard.

Charles and Emma Thompson, trading as Louise and Co. established their Bonnet
Box branch at 74–5 Shoreditch High Street before 1867 and this view is from their
prospectus of 1895. The business lasted in other hands until 1909, after which the
site was incorporated into Jeremiah Rotherham's hosiery emporium.

Shoreditch High Street looking north from just north of the Holywell Lane junction in 1896. Stall holders are out in force for the Saturday morning trade, selling everything from fruit and cockles to old books and live birds. On the left is drapers A. Lynes, whose catalogues were given to flights of verse. In the distance is the bulk of Rotherham's premises, and beyond are the towers of the London Music Hall.

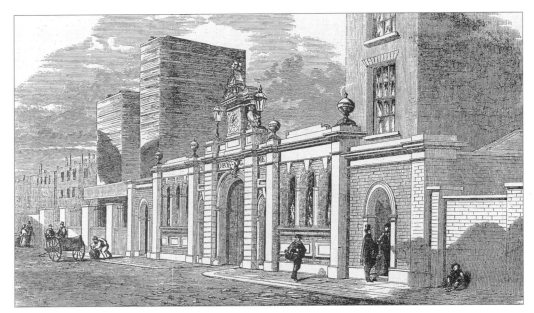

There were three gasworks in Shoreditch. The Gas, Light & Coke Co. built one in 1813 on the north side of Curtain Road, which was demolished in 1872. The Imperial's works at Whiston Street of 1824 had the gasholder destroyed by a V bomb in 1944 and the site was cleared by 1961. The Independent's works just south of the canal near Kingsland Road of 1824 were closed in 1908. Croll's gas meter works had been set up in 1859 on the Kingsland Road frontage (above); this and the remainder of the site then went over to stove and meter making, and the lower view shows the gas meters being made about 1930.

# 10. FROM 1900

In 1900 the vestries in London were abolished and replaced by metropolitan boroughs, with a mayor, aldermen and councillors. Shoreditch took as its new badge the coat of arms of John of Northampton, a fourteenth century Lord Mayor of London and a lord of one of the Shoreditch manors, adding the motto 'More Light, More Power' to emphasise local pride in the new electricity undertaking. The new council continued to develop services for its people; including a second public swimming bath, opened on Whiston Road in June 1904. There was little that could be done about the lack of open spaces, but the Council built on the work of the vestry and by the mid-1920s maintained the formerly private gardens in Charles and Hoxton Squares.

Shoreditch was also one of the founding authorities of municipal insurance. The Council hosted a meeting of representatives from nine boroughs, including the playwright George Bernard Shaw, and in 1903 the Municipal Mutual Insurance Company was established, operating from a basement room in Shoreditch Town Hall. The Council had extended the Town Hall in 1901, but during re-decorations in 1904 a catastrophic fire destroyed the interior of the meeting hall and the whole roof. The newly formed company was hard-pressed, but met the claim, thus firmly establishing its reputation with local authorities and beginning a growth that has only recently been ended.

The most notable local politician in the early twentieth century was Henry Busby Bird, who served as mayor from 1903–5, 1907–8 and 1910–19 and was knighted for his services in raising a local battalion of the Middlesex Regiment in the First World War. The Labour Party gained control in 1919 and with the exception of the years 1922–5 and 1931–4 ran the Council thereafter. Labour councillors included William and Henrietta Girling, whose joint service amounted to eighty-eight years. William Girling served as a local representative on the Metropolitan Water Board and has a reservoir named after him. Most influential in Labour's ranks was probably Dorothy Thurtle, daughter of Labour leader George Lansbury and whose husband Ernest was the MP for Shoreditch and Finsbury. In contrast to neighbouring Hackney, Shoreditch took little part in preparations for civil defence in the mid-1930s and this may have been due in part to the strong pacifist beliefs of Lansbury and his supporters.

Housing remained the largest single problem to face the authority. In the early 1920s over half of the population were still living in overcrowded conditions – nearly a quarter of

Shoreditch's population lived two to a room and the *New Survey of London Life and Labour* found that 60 per cent of what the authors termed 'working class housing' was overcrowded. The worst streets remained those around Nile Street, Essex Street and Wilmer Gardens. Both the London County Council and Shoreditch Council cleared streets and built new estates. Shoreditch built flats on New North Road and in the Teale Street area and also built cottages in Shap Street. Estates at Pritchard's Road and at Stonebridge (1923), were begun before the Second World War and extended afterwards. The Whitmore Estate, south of the Regent's Canal, was begun in 1927 and completed after the Second World War. Rehousing contributed to a further drop in population, from 118,637 in 1901 to 104,248 in 1921 and 97,042 ten years later. Major schemes like the redevelopment of the Dove Row area in 1938 displaced 2,400 people, of whom 1,000 were rehoused outside Shoreditch.

The inter-war years saw the development of welfare services, an extension of the public health inspection. After pressure from the Shoreditch Public Welfare Association (a temperance organisation formed in 1908), the Council adopted the Notification of Babies Act in 1909, leading to the employment of health visitors and the establishment of infant weighing centres. The Council worked with voluntary groups, including the Shoreditch School for Mothers, which by 1913 worked from three centres. From 1915 the Maternity and Child Welfare Centre at 152 Kingsland Road provided food and medical services for expectant mothers, and with the help of the Carnegie Trust a new centre opened in 1923. The Council also worked with other voluntary agencies. A nursery had been established in Shepherdess Walk before the First World War. In 1927 donations enabled this to be replaced with the Sun Babies Nursery in Felton Street, which provided a crèche for working mothers, medical services and vaccination and by the late 1930s was funding convalescent holidays for children. Financial problems led to Shoreditch Council taking over the nursery in 1941, keen to ensure that its facilities remained available to mothers and children in the war years.

The Shoreditch Public Welfare Association spawned two very active subsidiaries – a drama group, which revived the local connection with Shakespeare – and a housing association. After the demise of the SPWA in 1931 both became independent, and the Shoreditch Housing Association went on to build its first flats in Lyme Grove, Hackney, opened in 1934.

Much welfare provision came from voluntary agencies in the inter-war years. The Shoreditch Children's Outing Fund, founded in 1921, organised trips to Theydon Bois and Burnham Beeches for the poor and physically and mentally disadvantaged children. The Maurice Hostel Settlement, based at Herbert Street, with clubs in Shepherdess Walk provided clothes, food, toys and games and activities for mothers and children, with some activities for local boys and men, often on very limited funds. These were two among many agencies who provided support through the long period of high unemployment of the 1930s.

Shoreditch men had served in the First World War and many were killed or injured but the Borough largely escaped bombing. In contrast the Second World War saw sustained periods of bombing in 1940 and again from March 1941. The priest of St Augustine's

Church, Haggerston was one of many to shelter in Liverpool Street Tube station at night, standing for long periods in the heat with crowds and attempting to sleep on the platforms. The Borough played its part in local fund-raising, adopting a submarine, HMS *Thrasher* and using a model of it on a float to help fund war bonds. Many local businesses were bombed, especially in Shoreditch High Street, with wholesaler Jeremiah Rotherham's premises on the east side and Hill's tobacco works on the west being totally destroyed. Large areas of Father Wilson's parish were left in ruins and by 1945, there were numerous bomb sites and empty wildernesses where tightly-packed streets had once stood.

After the war, rehousing and migration had reduced the population to 44,871 by 1951 – less than half the 1931 total. Shoreditch Council pushed ahead with its slum clearance programme, demolishing older houses as well as using former bombed areas. By 1960 the Council was able to claim that its programme was largely completed, and over a third of the Shoreditch population now lived in council flats built either by Shoreditch or the London County Council. Other services were extended, including libraries. The Kingsland branch had been enlarged before the war, and the Pitfield Street Library, badly bomb damaged in 1941, was refurbished by 1956. Two smaller branch libraries were opened at Goldsmith's Row and Murray Grove. While the Pitfield Street baths, also bombed, were demolished and the electricity generating operation ceased after municipal electricity was included in the nationalisation programme of 1948, the damage to Whiston Road baths and laundry was made good. Shoreditch also launched its own local carnival in 1958, the decade that saw the beginnings of changes in the make-up of the population, with the arrival of immigrants from the West Indies and the Indian sub-continent.

Under local government re-organisation, Shoreditch Metropolitan Borough ceased to exist on 31 March 1965 and Shoreditch became part of the newly-created London Borough of Hackney. Since then many of the older businesses have closed and their premises divided into smaller workshops, especially in the southern area. Not all the cleared sites were redeveloped for housing, and two major new parks have been created; Shoreditch Park to the west of Pitfield Street, including the Britannia Leisure Centre, the first stage of which opened in 1980, and Haggerston Park. With relatively few tower blocks, much of the council housing has not been designated for demolition, unlike parts of Hackney to the north. In recent years the area has gained a reputation for the arts, with a jazz café and arts festivals and is shortly to see the opening of a major new community college incorporating a replacement library for the Pitfield Street one, which closed in 1995. With housing association property replacing much of the former St Leonard's Hospital in 1995 and City Challenge funds made available to repair and restore property around the Kingsland Road area, Shoreditch will have had a considerable face-lift by the end of the century. The former North London line to Broad Street closed in 1986 and the Broadgate Development obliterated the former station and some streets to the north. But the remainder of the line will form a new tube connection to link up with the Victoria Line at Highbury, part of developments that may give Shoreditch a more prosperous future.

# THE QUEEN'S AFTERNOON IN THE EAST END
## A TOUR OF SLUMLAND IN SHOREDITCH

WITH A MITE OF A PATIENT
in the St. Leonard's Infirmary.

WAITING AND WATCHING FOR THE QUEEN
A typical window scene.

WITH ANOTHER TINY PATIENT
in the St. Leonard's Infirmary.

Queen Mary's visit to Shoreditch on 25 March 1922 included the Gosling family home at 13 Ware Street, on the west side of Kingsland Road, from whence she has just emerged, escorted by the Mayor of Shoreditch.

Shoreditch's Model Welfare Centre on Kingsland Road was opened in 1923. These two views were taken for the 1937 Borough guide.

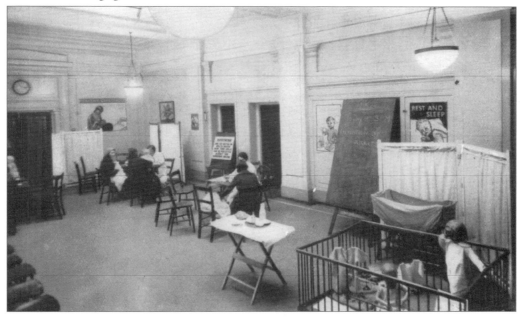

Shoreditch was keen to promote conversion to electricity, since the Borough was responsible for generation, and like other local authorities offered a wiring rental system to eliminate the capital costs of connection for customers. The lorry has all the latest appliances of 1926.

The courtyard of the Sun Babies Nursery, in Felton Street, 1937.

The booking office of Shoreditch station, on the corner of Old Street and Kingsland Road in 1926. Opened in 1865, the original station was demolished in 1927 when Kingsland Road was widened. War damage brought about the closure of the station in 1940, though the replacement booking office survives.

The view from the top of Belmont Mansions, Goldsmith's Row looking west, with St Augustine's Church roof in the centre. The open space was formerly the sites of Maidstone Street and the eastern side of part of Boston Street, some indication of the devastation suffered by Shoreditch. A view from about 1944.

One of the new London County Council estates, was the Whitmore Estate, begun in 1927 and in the course of completion when this view – showing the Kingsland Road block – was taken for the 1937 borough guide.

One of the last major clearance schemes undertaken by Shoreditch was at the top end of Pitfield Street. This view is taken from the site of the present roundabout in 1951. Anderson's survived to move into new premises on the same site after redevelopment.

Hoxton Street market in 1948 – a view taken to illustrate potential public health problems. Anyone for rabbit?

Hackney City Farm was founded in 1984 at the edge of Haggerston Park, bringing back livestock to an area that saw the last of its farms 160 years before, and the elimination of cow-keeping for local dairies in the 1930s. Pig racing is usually an annual event, and this view was taken in 1987.

# INDEX

Note: Subject entries are given under the Shoreditch heading and illustrations are marked in bold.